The Voice of God in the Present Hour

The Voice of God in the Present Hour

R. A. Torrey

AMG
PUBLISHERS

Chattanooga, TN 37421

The Voice of God in the Present Hour

Originally published by

Fleming H. Revell Company

ISBN 0–89957–248–0

Library of Congress Catalog Card Number: 98–87863

Printed in the United States of America

03 02 01 00 99 98 –B– 6 5 4 3 2 1

Contents

Preface

I have received urgent requests, especially from evangelists and ministers, to publish another volume of sermons. This volume is a response to this request. Quite a number have asked for publication of different sermons preached in The Church of the Open Door in Los Angeles. Many are included in this collection. It is the hope and prayer of the writer that they will not only be blessed to those who read them, but also that the material found in them may be used by others in preaching and teaching the truth of God. It has been a great joy to the writer that so many evangelists and preachers have used so generously material found in his previous volumes of sermons. Sometimes such use has not been acknowledged; but it frequently has been acknowledged and, even when not acknowledged, I have reason to think that great good has been accomplished by the truth thus given. Indeed, I have reason to know that some have used the material found in my sermons with an effectiveness far beyond that with which I used it myself, and it has been a great joy to me to have it thus used. As the purpose of the publication of these sermons is the convincing of unbelievers, the salvation of sinners, and the confirmation and guidance of God's people, it does not matter at all to me whether there is any acknowledgment on the part of those who use the material or not. If good is done, and I know much good is done, I therein greatly rejoice (Phil. 1:18).

R. A. TORREY

Los Angeles, Cal.

1

Not a Word of Christ
Shall Ever Fail

Heaven and earth shall pass away, but my word shall not pass away
(Matt. 24:35).

J esus Christ here asserts that His words are more stable and enduring than heaven or earth: that while heaven and earth shall pass away, His word shall not pass away. When we consider the position that Jesus Christ occupied when He made this extraordinary claim, it appears absurd in the extreme. He was an uneducated artisan of an obscure and despised people. Furthermore, it was only a few days before His crucifixion. The man who uttered these words in less than a week was to be the butt of the scorn and ridicule of jeering mobs as He ended His life as a condemned malefactor on a gibbet, only a short walk from where He was now speaking. If these words spoken by such a man, at such a time, prove true, then He must be more than appears at first sight. Indeed, He must be as He claimed to be, divine. Heaven and earth are God's own handiwork, and if Christ's words prove more stable than they, then He Himself must be divine.

I. Christ's Words Are Sure

But these remarkable words of Christ after the lapse of more than eighteen centuries are proven to be true. This stupendous claim of Christ that not a word of His shall ever fail has been substantiated. That the words of Jesus Christ shall never pass away is proven by the tests that they have already stood.

1. First of all, *the words of Jesus have stood the test of bitterest opposition.* No sooner had Christ's words fallen from His lips than they were hated. They have been hated through the nearly nineteen centuries that have elapsed since they were spoken. This hatred has been most bitter, most relentless, most energetic, most skillful, most wily, most powerful, but it has been utterly ineffective. This hatred manifested itself in literary attacks upon the words of Christ, like that of Lucian the great master of satire in his day, in philosophical attacks like that of the great philosopher Porphyry, in learned attacks like that of the scholar Celsus, in physical attacks like that of the great Roman Emperor Diocletian, in which he summoned all the political and military forces of the empire with torch, and stake, and prison, and wild beast to obliterate from the pages of history the memory of Jesus Christ and His words. From those early days to this, this opposition has gone on, more than eighteen centuries of it. All the artillery of science, literature, philosophy, political intrigue, sarcasm, ridicule, worldly ambition, force, all the artillery of earth and hell, have been trained upon the words of Christ, and for centuries at a time an almost incessant cannonade has been kept up. Sometimes weak hearts have been shaken by the roar of battle, but the words of Christ have remained absolutely unshaken. There has not been one single stone dislodged from these fortifications. Words that can come out of eighteen centuries of such experience as that unscathed, unscarred, unmarred, will stand forever. Heaven and earth shall pass away, but the words of Christ shall not pass away.

2. In the next place, *Christ's words have not only stood the test of bitter opposition, but they have also stood the test of time.* The test of time is a severe test of men's utterances. What seemed like wisdom when uttered a few years ago is seen today to be consummate folly. Ptolemy was by far the greatest astronomer of antiquity, and his utterances were considered the sum of all wisdom, but they have not stood the test of time, and his theories are today the laughing-stock of the schoolroom. What is true of the words of Ptolemy is true of all other books of the past but one; they are outgrown, but the utterances of Jesus Christ are not outgrown, they are as precious today as in that long-ago time when they were first spoken. They are as perfectly applicable to present-day needs as to the needs of that day. They contain the solution of all modern individual and social problems; they have perpetual youth.

There is not one single point at which the teachings of Jesus Christ have been outgrown or become antiquated. The human mind has been expanding for more than eighteen centuries since Jesus Christ spoke here on earth, but it has not outgrown Him. Words that can endure eighteen centuries of growth and still prove as thoroughly adequate to meet the needs of the race and each member of it as when first given will stand forever. Heaven and earth shall pass away, but the words of Jesus Christ shall not pass away.

Let me say in passing that in the light of history it is nothing short of preposterous, and even ludicrous, to hear men put forward the claims of the newly hatched philosophies of a day against the utterances of Jesus Christ that have stood the test of more than eighteen centuries, especially in view of the well-known fact that just such philosophies, full of self-confidence, have appeared by the thousands in the past, and after a brief day of notoriety have flashed out again into the darkness from which they had so recently emerged. The history of eighteen centuries of human thought is largely a history of men who counted themselves wiser than Christ, but whom it took only a few years to prove utter fools.

3. *The words of Christ have stood* a third test, *the test of rigid scrutiny.* No other words have ever been so examined, scrutinized, analyzed, pulled to pieces, subjected to the most minute, microscopic and unsparing examination, as have the words of Christ. They have undergone eighteen centuries of scrutiny, and what is the result?

a. The first result is, *not one single flaw has been discovered.* What would not men give to find one real flaw in the words of Jesus? What would not Ingersoll have given in his day? What would not some of our liberal teachers who would like to set themselves up by putting Jesus Christ down, give? What would not some of our professedly orthodox preachers, who care far more for a petty reputation for originality and advanced scholarship than they do for the untarnished splendor of the Son of God, give? They have searched for a flaw—generation after generation of the enemies of Christ. One generation failing to find such a flaw has bequeathed the search to another, and this search has gone on for more than eighteen centuries with the best microscopes that could be devised, and the search has failed, utterly failed. The words of Jesus stand out absolutely flawless. The words that have stood eighteen centuries of such scrutiny will stand forever. Heaven and earth will pass away, but the words of Jesus Christ shall not pass away.

b. But there is a second result of this scrutiny: *the words of Christ have not only proven themselves flawless, but inexhaustible.* These eighteen centuries have not only been centuries of scrutiny, they have also been centuries of profound, earnest, and honest study as well. Men have dug and dug for eighteen centuries into this mine of precious metal that they have found in the words of Christ. Thousands and tens of thousands have dug, and the mine has proven absolutely inexhaustible. There is more for the new miner that comes today than there was for the first digger. Eighteen centuries of digging and discovery and no hint of touching the bottom of the mine. The bottom is farther off than ever. The mine that has endured eighteen centuries of such digging and not given out never will give out. With the confidence born of eighteen centuries of experience, we can shout, "Heaven and earth shall pass away, but the words of Jesus shall not pass away."

4. *The words of Jesus Christ* have stood another test, *the test of history, measuring the accuracy of His prophecies.* Jesus Christ was a prophet. He undertook to tell the things that were to be. History is the touchstone of prophecy. The prophet who is not of God falls before the test of history, but Jesus Christ stands. Jesus Christ, while Jerusalem and the temple were still standing in their pride, magnificence and seeming security, foretold that the armies of Rome would come and besiege the city, that there would be a siege of such horror as was absolutely unparalleled in history; that not one stone should be left upon another, and that for long periods of time to come Jerusalem would be trodden underfoot of the Gentiles. So it has come to pass to the letter, and so it is being fulfilled even to our day. Jesus foretold that the Jew, though crushed, scattered throughout the earth, subjected to unparalleled tyranny, would preserve his race identity until Christ should come again. Centuries have rolled on, nations have arisen, fallen, been obliterated and forgotten, the Jew has not had a foothold anywhere for centuries, yet the Jew retains his race identity to this day as perfectly as he possessed it in the first century. It is the miracle of history, and the words of Christ stand. Jesus Christ predicted furthermore that the little church He was founding of obscure men in that obscure corner of the earth would spread throughout the earth

until the nations of the earth took shelter under the branches thereof. The prediction seemed utterly wild and preposterous, but it has come true. The words of Christ have stood the test of history. He predicted furthermore that His church having spread thus outwardly, corruption would begin inwardly and that this corruption would spread "until all was leavened." It was a passing strange prediction to make about one's own kingdom, but it has been fulfilled to the letter. The apparently preposterous and impossible words of Christ have stood the test of more than eighteen centuries of history. The words of prophecy that can stand the rigid test of eighteen centuries of history will stand forever. Heaven and earth shall pass away, but Christ's words shall not pass away.

5. *The words of Christ have stood the test of more than eighteen centuries of practical application.* Through these more than eighteen centuries men and women have had these words of Christ before them to live by if they would, and thousands and tens of thousands, hundreds of thousands, millions, have decided that they would. Men and women have tested the words of Christ, His promises, His moral precepts, His commandments, His warnings, in all the relations of life. They have tested His promises and His precepts in the home, they have tested them in the church life, in the place of business; they have tested them in prosperity and in adversity; they have tested them in sickness and in health; they have tested them in the joys of peace, and in the horrors of war; they have tested them in life, and when face to face with death; they have tested them in the sweet fullness of the unbroken family circle, and in the desolation when every earthly friend has been taken away. For eighteen centuries men have tested these words of Christ from the cradle to the grave, and the words of Christ have stood the test. They never fail, they never will fail. In all, these words of Christ have stood millions upon millions of tests and not one single case of failure. What may we say then without the shadow or the shade of a doubt? Not one word of Christ shall ever fail. Heaven and earth shall pass away but the words of Jesus Christ shall not pass away.

If there is anything absolutely sure, it is the words of Jesus Christ. Heaven and earth may pass away, they are material and subject to the changes and decay that are always going on in matter. They have stood for ages, but they will not always stand. There was a time, as both the Bible and science tell us, when the heavens and earth did not exist, and there will be a time when they do not continue to exist in their present form; but Christ's words are spiritual not material, unchanging not changing, eternal not temporal, and while the endless ages of eternity roll on they will still endure. Heaven and earth shall pass away, but the words of Jesus Christ shall not pass away.

II. Some Other Things That Are Sure Also

We see that Christ's words are absolutely sure. Not one word of His shall ever fail. But, if Jesus Christ's words are sure, some other things are sure also.

1. *It is sure that there is a future eternal heaven and eternal hell.* This, Jesus Christ plainly declares. The doctrines of an eternal heaven and an eternal hell are not speculations of the theologians, but proclamations of the Son of God. Jesus says that at His coming again all nations then living on the earth shall be gathered before Him and He shall separate them one from the other as a shepherd separateth his sheep from the goats, and that He shall set the sheep on His right hand and the goats to the left, and of those on the left hand He says, "These shall go away into eternal punishment: but the righteous into eternal life" (Matt. 25:31–34, 41, 46). Remember that these are not the words of some "antiquated, medieval, bigoted theologian," they are the words of the Son of God, the words of Him not one word of whom shall ever fail.

2. *It is sure again that anyone who believes in Jesus Christ shall receive forgiveness of sins and eternal life, no matter how greatly nor how long he may have sinned.* Jesus says that He "has power on earth to forgive sins" (Mark 2:10). He says again, "As Moses lifted up the serpent in the wilderness, even so must the Son of man be lifted up: that whosoever believeth in Him may have eternal life" (John 3:14, 15). These words seem incredible. They seem too good to be true, but Jesus Christ is the speaker and not one word of His shall ever fail. The heavens and the earth shall pass away, but His words shall not pass away. This statement that there is pardon and eternal life for anyone who will believe in Jesus Christ is absolutely sure. Is there anyone here tonight who is heartily sick of sin, and heartily tired of death? Come, believe on Jesus Christ and be saved and get pardon and eternal life tonight.

3. *It is sure* again that *no one who rejects Jesus Christ shall see life, but the wrath of God abideth upon him.* Men do not like that doctrine. They like to think they can reject Jesus Christ and yet be saved by their imagined morality, or in some other way. There is absolutely no foundation for such a hope. It is not the doctrine of "fierce old John Calvin" nor of "bigoted Jonathan Edwards," it is the declaration of Jesus Christ, who says in John 3:18, 19, "He that believeth on Him is not condemned: but he that believeth not is condemned already, because he has not believed in the name of the only begotten Son of God. And this is the condemnation, that light is come into the world, and men love darkness rather than light, because their deeds were evil." He says again in the 14th and 15th verses of the same chapter, "As Moses lifted up the serpent in the wilderness, even so must the Son of man be lifted up: that whosoever believeth in Him should not perish, but have everlasting life," the unmistakable implication of which is that the one who does not believe shall perish, no matter what else he may do, and John sums up the teaching of the Lord Jesus on this point by saying, "He that believeth on the Son hath everlasting life: and he that believeth not the Son shall not see life; but the wrath of God abideth on him" (John 3:36). Before you dare question the statement to your own eternal ruin, remember who makes it, the One not one of whose words shall ever fail.

4. There is another thing that is absolutely sure, it *is sure that if a man is not born-again, he shall not enter into the kingdom of God.* This is the word of Jesus Christ who says in John 3:3, 5, "Verily, verily, I say unto thee, except a man be born again, he cannot see the kingdom of God." And again, "Verily, verily, I say unto thee, except a man be born of water and of the Spirit, he cannot enter into the kingdom of God." It becomes a matter of tremendous importance to each one of us that we know whether we have been born-again. Heaven and earth shall pass away, but Christ's words shall not pass away, and Jesus Christ says that no one who has not been born-again shall enter His Kingdom. Oh man, oh woman, have you been born-again?

5. Still another thing is sure: *it is sure if one seeks to be a Christian without letting the world know it, seeks to be a Christian in the privacy of his own heart, it is sure that Jesus Christ will not acknowledge such a disciple when He comes.* His words on this point are very plain. He says in Mark 8:38, "Whosoever shall be ashamed of me, and of my words,

in this adulterous and sinful generation, of him also shall the Son of man be ashamed when He cometh in the glory of His Father, with the holy angels." And again He says in Matthew 10:32, 33, "Whosoever therefore shall confess me before men, him will I confess before my Father which is in heaven. But whosoever shall deny me before men, him will I also deny before my Father which is in heaven." Your own deceitful heart may seek to make you think that you can be a Christian and not tell it. False friends may try to persuade you of the same thing, but He, not one word of whose shall ever fail, says, "*Whosoever* shall be ashamed of me, and of my words, of him also shall the Son of man be ashamed, when He cometh in the glory of His father with the holy angels." Your opinions will pass away; your friends' false arguments shall pass away, heaven and earth shall pass away, but Christ's words shall not pass away.

Study Questions

1. How have Christ's words stood the test of better opposition?
2. How have Christ's words stood the test of time?
3. How have Christ's words stood the test of rigid scrutiny?
4. In what ways are the words of Christ a "mine"?
5. How have Christ's words stood the test of history?
6. How have Christ's words stood the test of practical application?
7. List some truths we can be sure of.

Wherein the Bible Differs from All Other Books

Sermon to the Graduating Class of Bible Institute of Los Angeles, June 25, 1916.

The prophet that hath a dream, let him tell a dream; and he that hath my word, let him speak my word faithfully. What is the straw to the wheat? saith the LORD (Jer. 23:28 RV).

The Bible stands absolutely alone. It is an entirely unique Book. All other messages compared with the message of the Bible are as chaff as compared with wheat. The attempt to compare the Bible with other books as if it were one of a class, possibly the best of the class, arises either from ignorance or thoughtlessness, or else from the fixed determination to do the Bible an injustice. We shall see this morning that there is none like it. The Bible is not a book, it is the Book. It is an often repeated incident that Sir Walter Scott, when he was dying asked his son-in-law Lockhart to read to him, and that Lockhart asked, "What book shall I read?" to which Sir Walter Scott replied, "There is but one book." Beyond question Sir Walter Scott was right. But someone may challenge that statement that the Bible stands absolutely alone as an entirely unique Book. Anyone has a perfect right to challenge the statement and demand wherein the Bible differs from all other books, and this morning I propose to take up the challenge and answer the question.

I. In Its Depth

First of all the Bible differs from all other books in its depth. The Bible is unfathomable and inexhaustible. It is unfathomable not because of the obscurity of its style, but because of the profundity of its teaching. No other book is more simple in its style than the Bible. Its style is so simple and clear that a child can understand it, but its truth is so profound that we explore the Book from childhood to old age and can never say we have reached the bottom. However deep we may go there are always deeper depths beneath. For eighteen centuries many of the greatest minds the world has ever known have been sounding its depths, but the bottom is not yet reached. Men of the greatest possible intellectual reach and power have devoted a lifetime to the study of this Book, but what man has ever dared to say or dreamed of saying, "I know now all that the Bible contains." If any man should say that he would be unanimously voted a sublime egotist or an egregious simpleton. Whole generations of scholars have devoted their lives to the study of this Book, each generation having the advantage of the labors and researches and discoveries of preceding generations, but can even the latest generation say, "we have discovered it all now, there is nothing left in the Bible for the next generation to discover"? The whole human race has been unable not only to exhaust, but even to fathom this Book. Well may we exclaim with the Psalmist, "Thy judgments are a great deep" (Ps. 36:6). The judgments of God, God's thoughts as revealed in this Book, are beyond any man and beyond any generation of men. They are beyond the whole race. This Book, like God's other book, the book of nature, and unlike any book of man, is unfathomable and inexhaustible by men. This fact, if it stood alone would be sufficient proof of its divine origin.

1. *There are whole volumes of meaning in a single and apparently simple verse.* A single verse of Scripture has often formed the basis upon which a literature of many volumes, both of prose and poetry, has been erected. This is true, for example, of John 3:16, "For God so loved the world, that He gave His only begotten Son, that whosoever believeth in Him should not perish but have everlasting life." It is true of 1 John 4:8, "God is love." It is true of Psalm 23:1, "The Lord is my shepherd; I shall not want." What single utterance of any other book could be the foundation of so much thought and expression as

these utterances of the Bible. Who but God could pack so many volumes into one little verse, or part of a verse?

2. *The Bible is always ahead of man.* The world is certainly making progress in its thinking. It is constantly leaving behind the scientists, philosophers, and sages of the past. But the world never leaves the Bible behind. It has never caught up with it. Show me a man who says he has outgrown the Bible and I will show you a man every time who is ignorant of the Bible and is talking of what he knows nothing about. Whence comes this Book which is always ahead of the age?

What other book ought to command the attention, the time, and the study that this Book does, which is deeper than all other books, ahead of all other books, and ahead of every age. You study today the latest things in science and it will be out of date in less than ten years, but the Bible is never out of date. If you wish to be not only abreast of the times, but ahead of the times, study the Bible. Jesus was ahead of His times because He studied so much of the Bible as then existed. Paul was ahead of his times for the same reason. Huss, and Wycliff, and Luther, John Knox, and Wesley, and Finney, and Moody were ahead of their times simply because they sought their wisdom from this Book.

II. In the Absolute Accuracy of Its Statements

The Bible differs from other books in the second place in the absolute accuracy of its statements. The Bible is the only Book that always says all that it means to say and never says anything more than it means to say. The more rigidly one examines the Bible and the more closely he studies it, the more will he be filled with admiration for the accuracy with which it expresses the truth. It never overstates, it never understates the truth. There is not one word too many and not one word too few. It is the model witness: it tells "the truth, the whole truth, and nothing but the truth." A very large part of man's difficulties with the Bible comes from not noting exactly what it says. Time and time again men have come to me and said, "I cannot believe this which the Bible says," and then have quoted something which they supposed the Bible said. But I have replied, "the Bible does not say that," and when we have looked it up, lo, it is some minute modification of what the Bible really says that has given rise to the difficulty. The Bible is always so absolutely exact, that I have found the best solution for very many apparent difficulties in the Bible to be to take the difficult verses precisely as they read.

III. In Its Power

In the third place the Bible differs from all other books in its power. There is perhaps no other place where the supremacy and solitariness of the Bible shines out as in its power. Colonel Ingersoll once said in Chicago that the money expended in teaching the supernatural religion of the Bible was wasted, and advised the ministers to "take for a series of sermons the history of the philosophy, of the art, and the genius of the Greeks. Let him tell," he continued, "of the wondrous metaphysics, myths, and religions of India and Egypt. Let him make his congregation conversant with the philosophies of the world, with the great thinkers, the great poets, the great artists, the great inventors, the captains of industry, and the soldiers of progress." This suggested scheme of Col. Ingersoll's was no new scheme, it has been tried over and over again, and I challenge any man who has eyes and is honest to say that the pulpits that have tried it have the same power to elevate, save and gladden, that the pulpits have that preach the supernatural religion of the old Bible. The man who thus talks is either talking about something of which he has made no thorough and candid study, or else he is deliberately shutting his eyes to very evident facts. In either case he is playing the hypocrite in posing as a teacher.

In what directions does the Bible show a power that no other book or books possess?

1. First of all, in its saving power. Does it need any proof that the Bible has a saving power that no other book possesses, and that all other books together do not possess?

a. The Bible has a unique saving power in individual lives. What book or books can match the Bible's record of men and women saved from sin and vice in all their forms, saved from drunkenness, drugs, lust, greed, ruffianism, barbarism, meanness, selfishness, by the power of this Book? Worthless sots transformed into honest citizens and fathers; degraded prostitutes transformed into holy women of God; savages who drank blood from human skulls transformed into noble lovers of friends and foes; murderers transformed into ministering angels. Single verses of this Book have more saving power than all other books put together. John 3:16 has saved more men from sin to holiness, from degradation to honor, from bondage to the devil to sonship of God, than all books outside of the Bible. Try and account for it as you may, the fact stands and does not admit of a moment's honest denial or question.

b. But the saving power of the Bible is not limited to the lives of individuals. It has saving power in national life. Try to obscure the fact as you may, all that is best in America, Germany, and England is due to this Book, and in our own day nations have been lifted out of savagery into Christian civilization by this Book. If this Book had been heeded the awful cataclysm of war that is devastating Germany, France and England today would have been avoided. The undermining of faith in this Book is the real cause of the present murderous war with all its unspeakable and immeasurable calamities, atrocities and horrors.

2. But the Bible has not only a saving power that no other book possesses, it has also a comforting power that no other book possesses. What book like this can stay the human heart in sickness and adversity, and comfort it in the bereavement that takes from us the light of our eyes and the joy of our homes. There is no heart wound for which the Bible has not a balsam. I hold in my hand a New Testament that is very precious to me because it was the gift of my mother to my grandmother, my father's mother, which was the stay of her life in her closing years. On the title-page of this Bible is written in my mother's hand, "Earth has no sorrow that heaven cannot heal." This is true, but thank God something better is true, and that is, earth has no sorrows that the Bible cannot heal even in the life that now is.

3. Furthermore, the Bible has a joy-giving power no other book possesses. There is no other joy so great, so exceeding, so overflowing, and so enduring as those know who study and discover the truth contained in this Book. This is a fact that any of you can discover by observation, and better yet, that all of you can know if you will by blessed experience. There are many who have sought joy wherever it was to be found, in pleasure, in study, and in sin, and have at last found a joy in the Bible they found nowhere else. There is a countless multitude who have been lifted out of awful depths of despair into lofty heights of unutterable joy by the truths this Book contains, and the speaker of this morning is one of them.

4. The Bible has a wisdom-giving power that no other book possesses. "The entrance of thy words giveth light" (Ps. 119:130). I have known people of very meager educational advantages but who have studied the Bible, who have more wisdom in the things of greatest practical and eternal import than many very learned men who have neglected this Book of matchless wisdom.

5. The Bible has a courage-giving power no other book possesses. No other book has made so many and such peerless heroes, it has made them too out of most unpromising stuff. It has transformed beardless boys and tender maidens into heroes.

6. The Bible has a power to inspire activity that no other book possesses. It makes lazy men industrious; half alive men fully alive. There are said to be but two things of which a professional tramp is afraid, water and work, but I have seen the very tramp from whom I got this information transformed into a man of untiring industry by the matchless teaching of this Book.

IV. In Its Universal Adaptability

The Bible differs from all other books in its universal adaptability. Other books fit certain classes or certain types, or certain races of men, but the Bible fits men universally.

1. It fits all nations. No nation has ever been discovered that the Bible does not fit. Charles Darwin, the greatest naturalist of his day, thought he had discovered in the Terra del Fuegans a people the Bible would not fit, and frankly stated that missionary work among them would be in vain. His exact words written after his visit to Patagonia were, "Nothing can be done by mission work; all the pains bestowed upon the natives will be thrown away, they never can be civilized." But more humble believers in the universal adaptation of the Bible and the gospel it contains thought differently, and proved their faith and so thoroughly convinced Charles Darwin by facts of his mistake, that he became a regular subscriber to the funds of the society they represented.

2. The Bible not only fits all nations, but it fits all ages. It is the child's Book, the young man's Book, the Book of the middle-aged, and the Book of the old.

3. The Bible fits all classes. It fits the poor, and it fits the rich. It fits the palace, and it fits the garret. It fits the learned, and it fits the

ignorant. It fits the nobleman, and it fits the peasant. It fits Gladstone, and James D. Dana, and Romanes, and Neander, and it fits the man so illiterate that he can scarce spell out its words.

4. The Bible fits all experiences. It is the Book for the hour of gladness, and the Book for the hour of sadness; the Book for the day of victory, and the Book for the day of defeat; the Book for the day in which we have achieved the greatest moral triumph, and for the day when we have fallen deepest into sin; the Book for the day of clearest faith, and the Book for the day of darkest doubt; the Book for the wedding day and the Book for the day of funerals. There is not an experience in life wherein the Bible does not have the message which we most need. To that fact there are tens of thousands of people of all classes in many nations ready to testify. The testimony is from such a host of witnesses and such competent witnesses that the only one who can doubt it is the man who is bound he won't believe.

V. In Its History

The Bible differs from every other book in its history.

1. *The Bible has been hated as no other book.* No book has ever aroused the animosity of men of all classes as the Bible has. The Bible has been hated by rich men, and it has been hated by poor men. It has been hated by the scholar, and it has been hated by the fool. It has been hated by common people, and it has been hated by rulers, governors, and kings. No other book has so aroused the bitterest antagonism. Men of seeming moderation and kindness of heart have been aroused to such a pitch of hatred by the Bible that they became murderers and torturers of men, women, and children, for example, Marcus Aurelius Antoninus. Even in our own day kind fathers and tender husbands have been moved by hatred of this Book to brutal treatment of children and of wives who have been led to accept the truth it contains.

2. *It has been loved as no other book.* If it has been intensely hated it has still more been intensely loved, loved by all classes, loved by the rich and loved by the poor; loved by the illiterate and loved by the greatest scholars the world has ever known; loved by men digging in the ditch, and loved by men ruling on a throne. Men, women and tender children have gladly laid down their lives for this Book.

3. *It has been victorious as no other book.* Though the Bible has been so bitterly hated and so vigorously assaulted, it has come off a complete victor. Centuries of assault have served only to prove its indestructibility and confirm its power. Celsus, Porphyry, Lucian, Diocletian, Voltaire, Volney, Hume, Tom Paine, Wellhausen, Graf Kühnen, Cheyne, and an innumerable host have trained their mighty guns against this Book. They have brought to bear against it all the powers of science, philosophy, literary criticism, ridicule, force, political and military power, and every other form of power that they possessed, and all their assaults have come to nothing. The Bible has come off a complete victor in every conflict. Anyone who will take the pains to consult history will have no doubts as to the outcome of the present attacks upon the Bible. Individuals of the past have talked just as boastingly of what they would do with the Bible in a few years as do the individuals of today, and with far more show of reason. But their confident boasts proved empty and futile and as we recall them now in the light of the established facts of subsequent history they only move us to a pitying smile. Voltaire is dead and forgotten, but the Bible is still alive and marching on. Attacks on the Bible may do injury to a few weak individuals, principally callow young men and romantic young maidens in high schools, colleges and universities, who allow themselves to be thus robbed of the saving, comforting, joy-giving, ennobling power there is in the Bible, but they do not hurt the cause of truth, for they but prove anew the divine indestructibility of the imperishable Book of God.

VI. In Its Authorship

Finally, the Book differs from every other book in its authorship. Other books are men's books. This is God's Book. Much that has already been said proves this. Its inexhaustible depth proves it. Only an infinitely wise God can be the author of an inexhaustible Book. Its absolute accuracy proves it. Men understate or overstate: God alone always states things just as they are. Its divine power proves it. Only a book that comes down from God can lift men up to God as this Book does. Its universal adaptability proves it. Only the Creator of all men can make a Book that is fitted to all men and every need of these men. Its history proves it. Only God can make a Book so indestructible against assault, against human reasoning, and human philosophy as this. An omnipotent Book must have an omnipotent author. There are many other facts about this Book that prove its divine authorship, but these are enough. There is evidently a certain Infinite character about this Book that points unmistakably to the Infinite character of its author. What this Book says God says, and whoever speaks according to this Book speaks the message of God and God speaks through him. He is God's mouthpiece.

Study Questions

1. How does the Bible differ from all other books in its depth?
2. How does the Bible differ from other books in the absolute accuracy of its statements?
3. How does the Bible differ from other books in its power?
4. In what ways does the Bible have universal adoptability?
5. How does the Bible differ from other books in its history?
6. How does the Bible differ from other books in its authorship?

3

Is the Bible in Danger?

Heaven and earth shall pass away, but my words shall not pass away (Matt. 24:35).

Some weeks ago I preached on this same text, but we are going to approach it tonight from a different standpoint. The question before us is, is the Bible in danger? Our text asserts that it is not, and I propose to show you tonight some reasons why the Bible certainly is not in danger. There are two classes who think that the Bible is in danger: first, there are those who think it is in danger because they are glad to think so, because it gives their consciences some little consolation in a life of sin to think that the Bible will not stand. But there is another class who fear the Bible is in danger, and it is with great reluctance that they think that it is; they love the Bible, they would be glad to believe the Bible, but they are afraid the old Book must go. Let us then honestly face the question, Is the Bible in danger? I shall prove to a demonstration that it is not in danger. I will not deny that the Bible has enemies, and most able enemies, most persistent enemies. Eighteen years ago when Colonel Ingersoll suddenly died there were many who breathed a sigh of relief, for they thought that the most dangerous enemy of the Bible was gone. But Col. Ingersoll was not the most dangerous enemy of the Bible. There were more dangerous enemies of the Bible even during his lifetime than he himself was, and there are far more dangerous enemies of the Bible than he today. They are more dangerous because they do not make the mistake that he made of thinking that the world would accept caricature for argument, and ridicule for reason, and rhetoric for logic. They are more dangerous also because they do not come out into the open, as he did, and frankly avow themselves to be infidels. They claim, in some sense, to believe in the Bible, but all the while that they claim to believe in it they are seeking, consciously or unconsciously, to undermine the faith of others in the absolute inerrancy and authority of the Bible. The most dangerous enemies of the Bible today are the college professors and principals of high schools, and even theological professors who, while they claim to be endeavoring to establish faith upon a broader and therefore better basis, are all the time attempting to show that the Bible is full of errors and not in accord with the assured results of modern science and history. These enemies are legion, they are found practically everywhere, many of them are able men, and they have formulated a skillfully planned campaign against the Bible. Nevertheless the Bible is in no danger. There are six reasons why the Bible is not in danger.

I. Because the Bible Has Already Survived the Attacks of More Than 1800 Years

The attacks now being made upon the Bible are not something new. The Bible has always been hated and assaulted. The Bible's stern denunciation of sin, the Bible's uncompromising demand of a holy, unselfish, consecrated life, the Bible's merciless laying of human pride in the dust, have aroused for the Bible a more bitter hatred from men than any other book has ever met. No sooner was the Bible given to the world than it met the hatred of men and they tried to stamp it out by every method and instrument of destruction they could bring to bear against it. The arguments that are brought against the Bible today are not new arguments, all of them were met and answered long ago. I am not aware of one single new argument that has been brought forward against the Bible in the last ten years. The antagonists of the Bible have tricked out the old arguments in new and more attractive garments, but they are the same old arguments. The arguments brought forward by the most learned and most able enemies of the Book today are the very arguments that have been employed for more than a century. If anyone will take the trouble to read Tom Paine's *Age of Reason*, he will be amazed to discover how many of the positions which men persist in calling "the *new* views" of the Bible were exploited by Tom Paine in his *Age of Reason* more than a century ago. Dr. Howard Osgood, a great scholar, in a discussion with the destructive critics some years ago, read a statement of the positions of the destructive critics as he understood them, and then turned to President Harper and inquired if the statements that he had read were not fair statements of the positions they held. President Harper replied that they were, and then Prof. Osgood startled his auditors, and especially his opponents, by saying, "In this statement that I have just read of your position, I have been reading verbatim from Tom Paine's *Age of Reason.*" With all the researches and all the labored efforts to find something against the Bible, not one single new argument has been forged in the last twenty years. There have been times in the past when the Bible has seemed to be in more peril than today, but when the storm of battle was over and the smoke of conflict had cleared away from the battlefield, this old, impregnable citadel of God's eternal truth has been seen standing there absolutely unhurt and unscarred, and the battle has only served to illustrate how impregnable is the citadel. Those who fancy that they are going to destroy the Bible with their puny weapons, and those also who fear it is going to be destroyed, would do well to reflect upon its history. The Book that has so triumphantly withstood the terrific assaults of eighteen centuries is not likely to succumb in a day. Voltaire, a far more gifted, versatile and skillful enemy of Christianity than any enemy living today, once boasted, "It took twelve men to establish Christianity. I will show the world it takes but one to destroy it." But somehow or other it did not destroy as easily as he imagined it would. Voltaire has passed into history, and largely into oblivion, and he will soon pass into utter oblivion, but the Bible has gained in power, and the very room in which Voltaire wrote the words quoted has been packed from floor to ceiling with Bibles for distribution, owned by the British and Foreign Bible Society. The advance of research from excavations in Bible lands, the advance of historical investigation, and the advance of science, have all served to confirm the truthfulness of the Bible. For example, the unearthing and deciphering of the cuneiform inscriptions, and the Moabite stone have shown the truth of Bible statements that were once questioned by scholars. As another illustration, not so many years ago ridicule was heaped upon the Bible implication of the existence of a great Hittite people. The investigations of comparatively recent years have proven the Bible right, and the critics utterly wrong. The skeptics of my early years made merry over the Bible mention of light before there was a sun, but today every man of science knows that according to the generally accepted nebular hypothesis there was light, cosmic light, before the sun became a separate body, and he also knows that even after the sun had become a separate body and the earth had been thrown off from the sun and the moon from the earth, that such dense clouds surrounded the earth for a long period of time that no light either from the sun or moon could reach the earth, and that afterwards the clouds became thin and dissipated and then, and only then, in that day, or period, of the earth's history did the sun and moon appear as definite heavenly bodies, giving light upon the earth by day or night. A very few years ago the destructive critics ridiculed the 14th chapter of Genesis and its mention of Amraphel, whom they asserted was an altogether mythical character, and many of them asserted that Abraham himself was a mythical character, but inscriptions made by this very Amraphel, or to use the modern name Hammurabbai, have been discovered, and a code of laws issued by him has been found, a code of a very lofty character, and now instead of sneering at Amraphel as a mythical character, the critics are trying to make us believe that Moses derived his legislation from him. The greatest scientist that America produced in the nineteenth century, my friend and beloved instructor in geology, Prof. James D. Dana, said, "The grand old book of God still stands; and this old earth the more its leaves are turned and pondered, the more will it sustain and illustrate the sacred word." Eighteen centuries of triumphant history and eighteen centuries of accumulating confirmation show that the Bible is not in any peril.

II. The Bible Is not in Danger Because It Meets and Satisfies the Deepest Needs of Man in Every Generation

Arthur Hallam said, "I see that the Bible fits into every fold and crevice of the human heart." This is true, but more than this is true. The Bible has an answer to every cry of the human soul, a balm for every wound of the human heart, a supply for every need of man. What are the deeper needs of man?

1. First of all, *the need of pardon and peace*. We are all sinners. We may try to dispute or obscure that fact, but we all know it is true. The Christian Scientist may assert that there is really no such thing as sin, that sin is only "mortal thought," or "illusion," and yet the Christian Scientist himself shows that he really believes that there is such a thing as sin by his holding other men responsible for their wrong acts. New theologians of the Reginald Campbell type may assert that the supposed fall of man was a fall upward, and that even man when he gets drunk or goes into lust is seeking after God, but in our deeper moments we all know that this is utter nonsense. In our deepest moments we all know we are not right and, though we may try to question it, we also fear that there is a holy God to whom we shall have to give answer for this sinful life of ours, and even if there is not such a holy God we know we shall have to give answer to our own consciences, which, like Banquo's ghost, will not down. Man is a sinner. Every man is a sinner. The great question then is, is there any place where pardon from God and peace in our own consciences can be found? The Bible answers this all-important question. It tells us that pardon and peace can be found in Jesus Christ through His atoning blood, and when we seek pardon and peace in Him, we find that what the Bible says on this point is true. There are many on every hand who can testify that they have found pardon and peace in Jesus Christ to whom the Bible pointed them. Years ago in Chicago a woman came to me who had been in a very real hell for fourteen years. For fourteen years conscience had tormented her with the thought of the man into whose throat she had driven a dagger and killed him. Oftentimes in her agony she had gone down to Lake Michigan by night and thought of plunging into its dark waters to drown herself and thus be free from her accusing conscience, but she hesitated to do it for fear of the awakening that might lie beyond death. I pointed her to Isaiah 53:6 and she found pardon and perfect peace through the One who had borne in her place the murder she had committed. The last three days of week before last and the first two days of last week I was in Chicago again. The first day I was there this woman came to me with a smiling face and told me how happy she was in Christ, and time and again she came to me at the close of some of the meetings, telling me how God was using even her in service for Him. This Book has saved many a conscience-tortured one from suicide and despair.

2. The next need of man is deliverance from sin's power. Men are in the grip of sin, we all know that. They are unable to break away from the grip of sin. It is well enough to tell a man to assert his manhood, but it doesn't work. The very lecturer who tells men that they do not need a Savior, Jesus, to set them free from the power of sin, that all they need to do is to assert their manhood, has not asserted his own manhood and broken away from sin's grip. This slavery of sin is awful; the soul cries out, where is deliverance to be found? The cry of Paul in his failure and defeat is the universal cry of the thoughtful heart, "Oh, wretched man that I am, who shall deliver me out of the body of this death?" (Rom. 7:24). The Bible answers the question in John 8:36, "If the Son shall make you free, ye shall be free indeed." When we try it, we find it is true. How many men there are whom we know who have been saved from lives of drunkenness and sin by this Book? How many homes there are in Los Angeles and throughout the land that were once poor, and dirty, and quarrelsome, that today are clean and well supplied and loving through the influence of this Book? How many men and women have been saved from lives of sin by this Book? With this, contrast infidelity. Where is the man who has been saved from drunkenness by the power of infidelity? Where is the home that was once poor and dirty and quarrelsome that is today clean and well supplied and loving which has been made so by the power of infidelity? Where is the sinning woman who has been saved from a life of sin by infidelity in any form?

3. The next need of man is comfort in sorrow. We live in a world that is full of sorrow and bereavement. Families are broken up, dear ones taken away. Man needs consolation as he stands by the dying bed of wife or child or mother; he needs consolation as he looks into the grave into which the dearest one of earth has been lowered. Where can he find consolation in such an hour? In the Bible, and in the Bible alone. On October 19, 1894, five years after the Johnstown flood, I stood in Johnstown cemetery. I looked upon the graves of several thousand who were in one day, May 31, 1889, swept into eternity— 816 unknown ones lay in a single plot. I read the inscriptions on the tombstones. What stories of sorrow they told. There lay side by side a young mother and her baby child; in another place lay "father, 34 years; Anne, 10 years; Tommy, 6 years; Elmer, 2," and the rest of the family were left to mourn. In another place lay seven of one family

side by side. There was need of consolation in those days in Johnstown. Was there any place where it could be found? Yes, in the Bible,
and in Jesus Christ of whom the Bible tells. On one tombstone I read,
"Annie Llewellyn, died May 31, 1889, five years, three months, sev-
enteen days, 'Safe in the arms of Jesus.'" Was there any comfort in
that for those parents as they thought of their little one caught by the
swirling flood, tossed about mid trees and crashing ruins, buried at last
in the awful mass of drift and dying ones at the bridge? On the family tombstone mentioned above I read these words, "Be ye also ready,
for in such an hour as ye think not the Son of man cometh" (Matt.
24:44). I read not one single inscription from Tom Paine, Voltaire,
Col. Ingersoll, or from any infidel writer or speaker, ancient or modern. Why not? Because there is no comfort in them. A few years before his death Col. Ingersoll wrote recommending suicide as the
best refuge he could suggest in great sorrow and failure. The Bible has
something immeasurably better to offer.

4. *Man's next need is hope in the face of death.* We must all sooner
or later stand face to face with death, then the soul of man, unless it
has been burned out by sin, cries, Does this end all, is there no light
in the grave? The Bible again meets and satisfies this cry. Col. Ingersoll
once asked in a lecture delivered in Chicago, (October 13, 1894),
"Why did not He (Christ) say something positive, definite and satisfactory about another world? Why did He not turn the tear-stained
hope of heaven into glad knowledge of another life?" Then he answered his own question in this way: "I will tell you why. He was a
man and did not know." The audacity of such an answer to an intelligent audience with an open Bible, is amazing. To imply that
Christ did not tell something "positive, definite, and satisfactory
about another world." To imply that He did not "turn the tear-
stained hope of heaven into glad knowledge of another life," and then
try to account for His not doing so! Col. Ingersoll must have thought
that his hearers either had no Bible or else would not read it. Jesus said
in John 14:1–3, "Let not your heart be troubled: believe in God, believe also in me. In my father's house are many mansions; if it were
not so, I would have told you; for I go to prepare a place for you. And
if I go and prepare a place for you, I will come again, and will receive
you unto myself; that where I am, there ye may be also." Is not that
something positive, something definite, something satisfactory about

another world? Again Jesus says in John 11:25, 26, "I am the resurrection, and the life: he that believeth in me, though he were dead yet shall he live. And whosoever liveth, and believeth in me shall never die." Is not that something positive, something definite, something satisfactory about another world? Again He says in John 5:28, 29, "The hour is coming, in which all that are in the graves shall hear His voice, and shall come forth, they that have done good, unto the resurrection of life, and they that have done evil, unto the resurrection of judgment." That certainly is plain enough, though it is not very satisfactory to those who are living lives of sin. But has the critical Colonel himself ever said anything "positive, definite and satisfactory" about another world? He had a most excellent chance to do so if he had anything to say, when he stood beside the grave of his own brother, but his pathetic but hollow eloquence on that occasion served only to illustrate the utter hollowness and emptiness of skepticism. The Bible has given men courage to die bravely and triumphantly in all the ages of its history. Infidels sometimes die stolidly and clinch their teeth and face it out, but they never die joyously and gloriously.

We might go on and show other needs of man that the Bible meets, but enough has been said to show that the Bible meets the deepest needs of man. As long as man needs pardon and peace, as long as man needs deliverance from the power of sin, as long as man needs comfort in sorrow, as long as man needs hope in the face of death, the Bible is not in danger. Man will not give up to satisfy any number of keen satirists or carping critics or plausible reasoners, the Book that meets his deepest needs, that brings pardon and peace instead of guilt and remorse, that brings liberty, manhood and nobility instead of bondage to sin, that brings comfort in the darkest hours of sorrow, transforming the thunder-cloud into the rainbow, that inspires man with unquenchable hope in the face of death and its terrors.

III. The Bible Is Not in Danger Because There Is Nothing Else to Take the Place of the Bible

The Bible contains all the truth on moral and spiritual subjects that all other books together contain. It contains more than all other books put together, and it contains all this in portable compass. Not a truth on moral or spiritual topics that cannot be found for substance within the covers of this little book. Even infidels' best thoughts are stolen from this book. For example, Ingersoll once said, "The doctrine that woman is the slave, or serf of man—whether it comes from hell or heaven, from God or demon, from the golden streets of the New Jerusalem or the very Sodom of perdition—is savagery pure and simple." This statement is true, but where did Col. Ingersoll learn this doctrine of woman's equality with man? He either learned it from the Bible or from someone else who had learned it from the Bible. What is the first thing that the Bible says about woman? You will find it in Genesis 2:18, "And the LORD God said, it is not good that man should be alone; I will make him a helpmeet for him." Here in its opening chapters the Bible proclaims the equality of woman with man. It declares that woman is not "the slave, or serf of man," but his companion and equal. Ingersoll was all right in his doctrine about the equality of woman, but he was unfortunately 3,500 years behind the Book that he sought to hold up to scorn. Turning to the New Testament, he might have read in Galatians 3:28 the statement that in Christ Jesus "there is neither male nor female." He might have read again in Ephesians 5:25, "Husbands, love your wives, even as Christ also loved the church, and gave Himself up for it." Certainly there is no suggestion there that "woman is the slave or serf of man." And he might have read a few verses further down in verses 28 and 29, "So ought men to love their wives as their own bodies. He that loveth his own wife, loves himself. For no man ever hated his own flesh; but nourisheth and cherisheth it, even as the Lord the church." And then he might have read two verses still further down, "For this cause shall a man leave his father and his mother, and shall cleave to his wife, and they two shall be one flesh." All the respect and honor and love and care bestowed upon woman today, woman owes to the Bible. But not only can we find every truth in the Bible that we find elsewhere, but there is more truth in the Bible than all other literature put together, and it is in portable compass. In the lecture already referred to Col. Ingersoll proposed to give to the world another and better Bible in place of this one, but where is it? Listen to what he says: "For thousands of years men have been writing the real Bible, and it is being written from day to day and it will never be finished while man has life."

"All the wisdom that lengthens and ennobles life—all that avoids or cures diseases, or conquers pain—all just and perfect laws and rules that guide and shape our lives, all thoughts that feed the flames of love, the music that transfigures, enraptures, and enthralls, the victories of heart and brain, the miracles that hands have wrought, the deft and cunning hands of those who worked for wife and child, the histories of noble deeds, of brave and useful men, of faithful, loving wives, or quenchless mother-love, of conflicts for the right, of sufferings for the truth, of all the best that all the men and women of the world have said and thought and done through all the years.

"These treasures of the heart and brain—these are the sacred scriptures of the human race."

That sounds pretty, doesn't it? I challenge any man to say that this is not a masterpiece of diction. But after all it is only rhetoric. *Where is* this Bible of which Ingersoll spoke? People want a Bible that they can lay their hands on, that they can make use of, that they can carry with them. A poor man cannot very well carry a Carnegie library in his trunk, and it would not do him much good in the great emergencies of life if he could. But here in this Book we have a Bible that a man can carry in his pocket wherever he goes, and in this one small Book he has more of truth of eternal value than in all the libraries of the world. No, the Bible is not in any danger, for there is nothing else to take its place.

IV. The Bible Is Not in Danger Because It Has a Hold That Cannot Be Shaken, on the Confidence and Affection of the Wisest and Best Men and Women

The Bible has the distrust and hatred of some, but it has the confidence and affection of the wisest, and especially the holiest of men and women. The men who know the Bible best are the men who trust it most and love it best. A superficial knowledge of the Bible, such as Col. Ingersoll, for example, had, or Tom Paine had, or that many a college and even theological professor today has, may lead one to distrust it and hate it, but the deep and thorough knowledge of that Book comes from a pure heart, and profound study will always lead one to love and trust it. The Bible is distrusted and hated by those whose influence dies with them. The Bible is loved and trusted by those whose influence lives after them. Lucian, Celsus, and Porphyry were great men, but their influence died with them, but the influence of John and Paul lives on in ever-widening power. Voltaire and Volney were able men, among the ablest men of their day, but their influence belongs wholly to the past, but the influence of Whitfield and Wesley is greater today than when they were here on earth. Colonel Ingersoll was a man of brilliant gifts, but his influence has not lived after him. Indeed it is amazing how completely he has sunken out of sight in the eighteen years that have elapsed since his death. But the influence of Spurgeon and Moody is with us still. No, the Bible is not in danger, for it has the ever-increasing confidence of the best men and women, of those men and women whose influence lives after them, and only the distrust and hatred of those whose influence dies with them.

V. The Bible Is Not in Danger Because It Is the Word of God

I have not space to go into that at this time. Many things prove that the Bible is the Word of God: its fulfilled prophecies, its unity, its divine power, its inexhaustible depth, the fact that as we grow in knowledge and holiness—grow Godward—we grow toward the Bible. Just a moment on its fulfilled prophecies. Look at the 53rd chapter of Isaiah. This chapter has been the rock upon which infidelity has always gone to pieces. Men have tried to get around the force of the argument by the desperate expedient of saying that the chapter does not refer to Christ but to suffering Israel, but even one careful reading of the chapter will show that it cannot refer to suffering Israel. Look at Daniel 9:25–27 with its prediction of the exact time of the manifestation of the Messiah to Israel and its prediction of His death and what would follow. Look at Micah 5:2 and its prediction of the very place in which the Messiah should be born. Right before our own eyes in the last two years we have seen predictions from the Bible fulfilled that men said never could be fulfilled. They told us that wars were at an end forever, that man had made such progress in his evolution that a great war would never be possible again among civilized nations of the earth, and that the predictions of the Bible that greater wars and times of distress were coming than the world had ever seen were foolish and impossible of fulfillment, but today we see these prophe-cies being fulfilled before our very eyes. The other arguments to prove that the Bible is the Word of God I have not time to go into at all, but they are absolutely conclusive. The Bible is not in danger be-cause it is God's Book. "Heaven and earth may pass away but God's Word shall not pass away" (Matt. 24:25), or to put it as Peter puts it in 1 Peter 1:24, 25, "All flesh is as grass, and all the glory of man as the flower of grass. The grass withereth, and the flower thereof falleth away: but the word of the Lord abideth forever."

VI. The Bible Is Not in Danger Because Any Honest and Earnest Seeker after Truth Can Find Out for Himself That the Bible Is God's Word

In John 7:17 Jesus offers a test that any man can try for himself. He says, "If any man willeth to do his will, he shall know of the teach-ing, whether it is of God, or whether I speak from myself." Many have tried this test, and it has never failed. A few weeks ago at the close of one of our evening services a man came to me saying that he was full of doubts, that while he believed that there was a God, he doubted that Jesus Christ was the Son of God, or that the Bible was the Word of God. He said further, he had been advised to accept it on blind faith without evidence. I told him to do nothing of the sort. I told him that believing without evidence was not faith but credulity, and that God did not ask any man to believe without evidence. Then I gave him the passage just quoted, "If any man willeth to do his will, he shall know of the teaching, whether it is of God, or whether I speak from myself." I told him to surrender his will to God and then ask God to show him whether Jesus Christ was His Son or not, and whether the Bible was His Word or not, and to take the gospel of John and read it, not trying to believe it, but being willing to be convinced if it was true, and promising God that he would take his stand upon everything in it that he found to be true. Within a week I received a letter from this man telling me how he had come out into the clear light of faith in Jesus Christ as the Son of God. I have seen the man again today and not only has his own skepticism entirely vanished, but he is leading other skeptics to Christ.

The Bible is in no danger. As far as the Bible is concerned all these attacks from different sources upon the Bible do only good, they set people to thinking about the Bible, they set preachers to preaching about the Bible, they serve to illustrate the invincible truth and power of the Bible by showing the ease with which such fierce attacks upon it are repelled. But while the Bible itself is in no danger, those who vent their spleen upon it are in danger. It is no small sin to ridicule the Word of an all holy and almighty God. There are others also who are in danger, those who listen to the fascinating eloquence of gifted unbelievers and allow it to lull them to repose in a life of sin, they are in danger. Men, and especially young men, your consciences were once troubling you, and you were contemplating forsaking your folly, but you have allowed yourselves to be blinded by the voice of some brilliant agnostic, and you are now about to trample underfoot the Word of God and the Christ of God. Do not be deceived, these voices that speak to you are not the voices of truth but the voices of falsehood, infamous, dastardly, soul-destroying falsehood. To listen to these voices means ruin, eternal ruin. Do not listen to such voices; listen to the voice of God that speaks to you in wondrous love from this Book and says, "Let the wicked forsake his way, and the unrighteous man his thoughts: and let him return unto the LORD, and He will have mercy upon him, and to our God, for He will abundantly pardon." Yes, and there is another class in danger. All those who do not accept Jesus Christ are in danger. This Book is not in danger, every utterance of it will stand, and this Book declares in John 3:36, "He that believeth on the Son hath everlasting life: and he that believeth not the Son shall not see life; but the wrath of God abideth on him." It is true, and if you do not believe on Christ, if you do not speedily give up your unbelief and put your trust in Him, you must perish.

Study Questions

1. What are the six reasons why the Bible is not in danger?
2. What are the "deeper needs of man"?

4

Why I Believe That Jesus Christ Is God in Human Form

There is no subject more important than that of the Deity of Jesus Christ. If Jesus Christ is not God manifest in the flesh, then Christians are idolaters, for Christians worship Jesus Christ. If Jesus Christ is God, then all who do not acknowledge Him as such and accept Him as their divine Savior and surrender absolutely to Him as their divine Lord, and worship Him as God, are guilty of the awful sin of rejecting a divine person and robbing Him of the honor due to His name. It is then of the highest importance that each of us know whether Jesus Christ is God or not. I am to give you tonight some of the reasons why I believe that He is the Son of God in an entirely unique sense, the Son of God in a sense in which no other person is or ever was the Son of God, the Son of God in such a sense that all the attributes and perfections and glory of God dwelt in Him. There was a time when I doubted it; very seriously and very earnestly and very honestly doubted it. I doubt it no longer and will tell you why not.

I. I Believe That Jesus Christ Is the Son of God in an Altogether Unique Sense, the Only Begotten Son of God, in Such a Sense That God the Father Dwelt in Him in All the Fullness of His Attributes and Glory Because of His Own Claim to Be the Son of God and the Way in Which He Substantiated That Claim

There can be no honest doubt in the mind of any man who will study the subject candidly and carefully that Jesus Christ claimed to be the

Son of God in a sense in which no other was the Son of God. In the 12th chapter of Mark He speaks of all the prophets that had gone before Him, even the greatest of them, as servants of God, and of Himself as *the only* Son of God (v. 6, RV). In the 3rd chapter of John, the 16th verse, He speaks of Himself as the only begotten Son of God. In John 5:23 He claims all men should honor Him *"even as* they honor the Father." In John 8:24 He says, *"If ye believe not that I am He, ye shall die in your sins."* During His last hours before His crucifixion the Jewish high priest said to Him, "I adjure thee by the living God, that thou tell us whether thou art the Christ, the Son of God," and Jesus replied, "Thou hast said." This was the strongest form of affirmation, and He went on to emphasize what He had said by adding, "I say unto you, Henceforth ye *shall see the Son of Man sitting at the right hand of power,* and *coming on the clouds* of heaven." Now throughout the Old Testament the only one who made the clouds His chariot was Jehovah, and Jesus here affirms in the most striking way under oath that He is a divine person, that He is Jehovah. In John 14:9 He went so far as to say, *"He that hath seen me hath seen the Father."* From these and from many other utterances of our Lord, it is perfectly plain that the Lord Jesus claimed to be the Son of God in a sense that no other was the Son of God, in the sense that in attributes and authority and worthiness of worship He was on an equality with God the Father. HE CLAIMED TO BE DIVINE. But a claim to be divine does not prove one to be divine. Men rightly demand that such a claim be substantiated, and *I do not believe that Jesus Christ is divine simply because He claimed to be, but because of the way in which He substantiated the claim.*

Christ's Claim to Be Divine Is Substantiated.

1. *First of all by His character.* The beauty and strength and nobility of the character of Jesus Christ is well-nigh universally admitted. The Jew admits it, both Rousseau and Renan, the great French skeptics, insisted upon it, even Colonel Ingersoll spoke most beautifully of it. On one of his last visits to the city of Chicago he repeated what he had often said before, "I wish to say once for all that to that great and serene man I pay, I gladly pay, the homage of my admiration and my tears." But here is this man whom all admit to have been a good man, a man of honor, humility, truth, and nobility, claiming to be divine.

IF HE WAS NOT DIVINE HE WAS THE BOLDEST BLASPHEMER AND MOST ARRANT IMPOSTOR THIS WORLD HAS EVER SEEN. Can any honest man who has ever read the story of Jesus Christ with any attention and candor believe He was a blasphemer and impostor? That is the only alternative: you must either admit the lofty claims He made about His Deity, or hold Him to have been a blasphemer and an impostor. Every one who denies the Deity of Christ practically lays at His door the charge of blasphemy and imposture. Men sometimes say to me, "I do not believe that Jesus was divine, but I believe He was a good man." I reply, "No, if He was not divine, He was not a good man." If Jesus was not divine, He was rightfully put to death according to Jewish law. The manner of His trial was illegal, the mode of death by which He was executed was not that prescribed, but the death penalty was the right penalty according to Jewish law. The one who denies the divinity of Christ justifies His killing.

2. *Jesus Christ's claim to be divine is substantiated by the miracles which He performed.* Herculean efforts have been put forth to discredit the gospel stories of His miracles, but these efforts have all failed. It was first attempted to prove that these recorded miracles were simply natural events, but this attempt failed. It was then attempted to prove that the reports were fabrications, pious frauds, of Christ's disciples, but this attempt likewise failed. It was then attempted to prove that the gospels did not belong to the time of Christ's disciples, but were written at a later period and palmed off as the productions of men who did not really write them. This last attempt was made in a most skillful, laborious and scholarly way. For a time it almost seemed as if the attempt might succeed, but at the last it broke down utterly. The argument for the early date and historical accuracy of the gospel stories in the ultimate outcome was only brought out the more clearly by the attacks made upon them, and the argument is absolutely unanswerable. It is an interesting fact that the final and decisive blow in favor of the authenticity of the most important of the four gospels, the gospel of John, was struck by a Unitarian, Dr. Ezra Abbott. Dr. Ezra Abbott's demonstration of the Johannean authorship of the fourth gospel was written many years ago, but all attempts to answer it have failed utterly. The miracles then attributed to Jesus Christ He actually performed. But these substantiate His claim to be divine. Not that the mere performance of miracles proves one

to be divine, but when one claims to be divine and then performs miracles of the character that Christ performed, not merely healing the sick, but stilling the wind, calming the waves of the sea, raising the dead, casting out demons, by His mere word, these works taken in connection with His character and His teaching and His claims prove Him to be divine.

3. *Christ's claim to be divine is substantiated in the third place by His influence on the history of the world.* It needs no argument to prove that Christ's influence upon the history of the world has been beneficial immeasurably beyond that of any other who has ever lived. His influence upon domestic life, His influence upon social life, His influence upon industrial life, His influence upon political life. It would be foolish to compare that of any other man, or that of all other men together, with His. Other men have had as many or more followers than He, but what is the quality of the influence of these men? Go to Turkey and note the influence of Mohammed; go to India and Ceylon and Japan and note the boasted influence of Buddha; go to China and note the influence of Confucius. No, Christ has had an incomparably divine influence upon men of all succeeding generations. Now, as already seen, if Jesus Christ was not divine, He was a blasphemer and an impostor. Is it conceivable that an arch impostor should have such an incomparable influence over men in all the relations of life? The question needs no answer, it answers itself.

4. *Christ's claim to be divine is substantiated, in the fourth place, by His resurrection from the dead.* We have not time tonight to go at length into the argument for the truthfulness of the gospel stories of Christ's resurrection from the dead, but the argument is clear and conclusive. In my book, *The Bible and Its Christ*, I have taken up the argument for Christ's resurrection and shown how it is impossible for any honest man to study the argument for Christ's resurrection and come to any other conclusion than that Jesus really rose from the dead as is recorded in the four Gospels. Now the mere fact that one rose from the dead would not necessarily prove him to be divine, but when one claims to be divine and is put to death for making the claim, and before dying asserts that God will raise Him from the dead and thus endorse His claim, if then God actually does raise Him from the dead at the appointed time, certainly God does by that act in a most unmistakable way set His seal to the claim, and in this way God has in

fact set His seal to Jesus' claim to be divine. As Paul puts it in the epistle to the Romans, Jesus Christ was "declared to be the Son of God
with power by the resurrection from the dead" (Rom. 1:4). All these
things taken together are my first reason for believing Jesus Christ to
be divine, because of His own claim to be, and the way in which He
substantiated this claim, by His character, His miracles, His influence,
and His resurrection. The argument is a compound one, composed of
several strong strands, and when these strands are woven together
there results an argument that it is absolutely impossible to break.

II. I Believe Jesus Christ to Be Divine Because of the Other Teachings of the Bible Besides His Own

The Bible is the Word of God. I have given on many occasions my
reasons for believing the Bible to be the Word of God. (See book, *The
Bible and Its Christ.*) The argument for the divine origin of the Bible
is unanswerable. The Bible is the Word of God and therefore true.
Whatever the Bible says about Jesus Christ is the truth about Jesus
Christ. But the Bible in the most unmistakable terms declares Him to
be divine. The Bible ascribes divine attributes to Jesus Christ, it attributes divine works to Him, in the New Testament it applies passages
to Jesus which in the Old Testament are spoken of Jehovah, it cou-
ples the name of the Lord Jesus with the name of God the Father in
a way in which it would be impossible to couple that of any finite being
with that of the deity, and it demands for Him divine homage and worship. John tells us that his whole purpose in writing his Gospel was
that men might "believe that Jesus is the Christ the Son of God; and
that believing [they] might have life in His name" (John 20:31).
Paul tells us "that at the name of Jesus every knee [shall] bow, of things
in heaven and things in earth, and things under the earth; and that
every tongue [shall] confess that Jesus Christ is Lord, to the glory of
God the Father" (Phil. 2:10, 11). He is quoting here a statement made
in the Old Testament of Jehovah (Is. 45:21–23). In Romans 9:5
Paul unhesitatingly declares that Christ "is over all, God blessed
forever," and the author of the epistle to the Hebrews says, "When he
bringeth in the first begotten (that of course is the Lord Jesus, as the
context clearly shows) into the world, he saith, And *let all the angels
of God worship Him.*" The Bible then, in the clearest, most definite and

most decisive terms teaches the true deity of Christ; and therefore, I believe Him to be God in human form.

III. I Believe That Jesus Christ Is Divine, God Manifest in Human Form Because of the Divine Power He Possesses and Exercises Today

It is not necessary to go back to the miracles of Christ when upon earth to prove He has divine power. He exercises that power today, and anyone can test it.

1. *He has power to forgive sins.* He claimed this power when here on earth and the scribes accused Him of blasphemy for making the claim, and if He had not been divine they would have been right in accusing Him of blasphemy, but He silenced them by demonstrating the claim (Mark 2:5–12). He has the same power today. Thousands can testify that they came to Christ burdened with an awful sense of guilt and that Christ has actually given their guilty conscience peace, absolute peace.

2. *He has the power today to set Satan's victims free.* He sets the one chained by drink free from the power of drink; the one chained by opium or other drugs, free from the power of drugs. He sets the slave of lust free from the power of lust. You may say that Keeley sets the one chained by drink or the power of drugs free, but the cases are not at all parallel. Keeley uses drugs, Christ merely spoke a word. Thousands and thousands have been set free from the power of drink and transformed into noble men and women of God by the simple word of Jesus Christ. Christ sets free not merely from drunkenness and other vices, but from sin. He makes the impure man and woman pure. He makes the selfish man unselfish. He makes the devilish man and woman Christ-like. I believe Jesus Christ is divine because of the divine power I see Him exercising in the lives of many men and women. I know Jesus is divine because of the divine work that He and He alone has wrought in my own life.

IV. I Believe That Jesus Christ Is Divine, God Manifest in Human Form Because of the Character of Those Who Accept Him as Divine

Those who accept Jesus Christ as the Son of God are those who live nearest God, in most intimate communion with God, and who know

God best. Those who know God best and live nearest to God have no doubts whatever that Jesus Christ is His Son. The cry, "I do not believe Jesus to be the Son of God," never comes from those who are living nearest God and know God best. It comes most often from those who are living farthest from God and know God least. Those who once believed Jesus Christ to be the Son of God as they drift away from God into worldliness, selfishness and sin often find themselves questioning the deity of Christ. On the other hand, those who once questioned the deity of Christ when they come nearer to God, when they turn their backs upon sin and selfishness and give themselves up more wholly to find and do His will, find their doubts about the deity of Christ rapidly vanishing.

V. I Believe Jesus Christ to Be Divine Because of the Results of Accepting His Deity

The religion that accepts God the Father but rejects Jesus Christ as His Son has no such deep and lasting moral power as the religion that accepts Jesus Christ as divine. Unitarianism has always proved to be impotent. Unitarianism does not save the fallen. Wherever you find a rescue mission that is doing a real and permanent work in lifting up the fallen, you will always find it manned and womaned by persons who believe in Christ as the Son of God. Unitarianism can do philanthropic work, it can build hospitals and operate soup kitchens and various kinds of clubs for helping the needy, but it does not save. I do not mean merely that it does not save from hell hereafter, it does not save from sin here and now. It is the gospel *of the Son of God* that does this. Unitarianism never begets a missionary spirit. With all its members and wealth by a mighty effort it induced one man to go as a foreign missionary for a little while, but even that poor lone missionary soon returned. Faith in Jesus as divine makes missionaries and martyrs and produces men of prayer and faith, it produces consecrated living. The denial of the deity of Christ tends to prayerlessness, religious carelessness, unbelief, worldliness, selfishness, and easy-going living. There is a power in the prayers of those who approach God in the name of Christ that there is not in the prayers of those who reject His deity. While Mr. Moody was still in business, before he had taken up Christian work as his exclusive occupation, he often went out holding meetings. One time he was holding meetings in one of the smaller towns in Illinois, the wife of the district judge came to Mr. Moody and asked Him to speak to her husband. He replied, "I cannot speak to your husband. Your husband is a book infidel and I am nothing but an uneducated boot clerk from Chicago." But the wife was so insistent that Mr. Moody finally called upon the judge. As he passed through the outer office the law clerks tittered to themselves as they thought how the learned judge would make mincemeat of the uneducated boot clerk from Chicago. Mr. Moody said to the judge in the inner office, "Judge, I cannot talk with you, you are an educated man; I am nothing but an uneducated boot clerk, but I just want to ask you one thing. When you are converted will you let me know?" "Yes," the judge replied banteringly, "when I am converted I will let you know." And then he raised his voice louder and said, "Yes, young man, when I am converted I will let you know. Good-morning." As Mr. Moody passed into the outer office the judge raised his voice still louder so all the law clerks could hear, "Yes, young man, when I am converted I will let you know." And the law clerks tittered louder than ever. But the judge was converted within a year. Mr. Moody revisited the town and called upon the judge. He said, "Judge, will you tell me how you were converted?" "Yes," the judge replied,

one night my wife went to prayer meeting as usual, but I as usual stayed at home and read the evening paper. I began to get very uneasy and miserable, and before my wife returned from the prayer meeting I was so miserable I was afraid to face her and retired for the night. On her return, finding me in bed she came to the door and asked if I were sick. "No," I replied, "I am not sick, only I was not feeling very well. Good-night." I had a miserable night and was so miserable in the morning that I dared not face my wife at the breakfast table, and I simply looked in the door and said, "Wife, I am not feeling very well this morning, I will not eat any breakfast." I went to my office and told the clerks they could take a holiday. I locked the outside door and then went into my inner office and locked the door to that. I sat down, getting more and more miserable all the time. At last, in my misery and in my overwhelming sense of sin I knelt down and cried, "Oh, God, forgive my sins." But there was no answer. Again I cried, "Oh, God, forgive my sins." But still no answer. I would not say, "Oh, God, *for Christ's sake* forgive my sins," because I was a Unitarian and did not believe in the divinity of Christ. Again I cried, "Oh, God, forgive my sins," but still there was no answer. At last in desperation I cried, *"Oh, God, for Jesus Christ's sake forgive my sins,"* and instantly I found peace.

"By their fruits ye shall know them" (Matt. 7:20). There is a divine power in a faith that accepts Jesus Christ as the Son of God that there is not in a faith that denies His deity.

Jesus Christ is the Son of God. He is divine. He is God in human form. His own claims substantiated by His character, by His miracles, by His influence upon the history of the world, by His resurrection from the dead, prove it. The teachings of the Word of God prove it. The character of those who accept Him as divine proves it. The results of accepting Him as divine prove it. The divine power He possesses and exercises today proves it. Jesus Christ is divine, He is God in human form. And now someone will say, well what of it? Everything of it. Jesus Christ is the Son of God, and if you reject Him, you are rejecting the Son of God. That is the awful sin that lies at the door of every man and every woman in this audience, out of Christ, REJECTING THE SON OF GOD! If your hearts were not hardened and blinded by sin, you would tremble at that indictment (Acts 2:36, 37). In the light of the clear proof of the deity of Christ I call upon you tonight to accept Him as your divine Savior. I call upon you to surrender to Him as your divine Lord. I call upon you to submit your life to Him as your rightful sovereign, and to manfully confess Him before the world as your divine Lord.

Study Questions

1. How is Christ's claim to be divine substantiated?
2. List two ways in which Christ exercises His divine power today.

5

Jesus the Wonderful

For unto us a child is born, unto us a son is given: and the government shall be upon His shoulder: and His name shall be called Wonderful, Counselor, the mighty God, the everlasting Father, the Prince of Peace (Is. 9:6).

The prophet Isaiah with a mind illumined by the Holy Spirit, looked down 740 years and saw the coming of Jesus of Nazareth and uttered the sublime words of our text. In them is wrapped up a world of meaning concerning the divine glory, the matchless character, and wonderful offices of our Lord. But tonight we must limit our thought to one clause in this great verse, "His name shall be called Wonderful." In the Bible names have meaning, especially when applied to God the Father, the Son or the Holy Ghost. The *name* is a revelation of what one is. Jesus is called "Wonderful!" because He is wonderful. First Jesus is Wonderful in His nature; second Jesus is Wonderful in His character; third, Jesus is Wonderful in His work.

I. Jesus Is Wonderful in His Nature

First of all Jesus is wonderful in His nature.

1. *He is a divine being.* He is divine in a sense in which no other man is divine. The Bible, both the Old Testament and the New, is full of that great truth. He most unhesitatingly made the claim. In Mark 12:6, after speaking of the Old Testament prophets as *servants*, He speaks of Himself as the "beloved" *Son* of God, and "only" Son of God. In John 10:30 He says, "I and my Father are one." In John 14:9 He goes so far as to say, "He that hath seen me hath seen the Father," and

in John 5:23 He says, "All men should honor the Son even as they honor the Father." The apostle John said of Jesus in the opening verses of His gospel, "In the beginning was the Word, and the Word was with God, and *the Word was God. The* same was in the beginning with God. All things were made through Him; and without Him was not anything made that hath been made" (John 1:1–3). And further down in the 14th verse he says, "And the Word (that is this Word that was in the beginning and that was with God and was God) became flesh and dwelt among us (and we beheld His glory as of the only begotten of the Father), full of grace and truth." The apostle Thomas after the resurrection of our Lord, fell at the feet of Jesus and cried to Him, "My Lord and *my God*" (John 20:28). The apostle Paul said of Him that "In Him dwelleth *all the fullness of the Godhead* bodily" (Col. 2:9), and he says of Him again in Romans 9:5 that He "is over all, *God blessed forever.*" The apostle Peter in Acts 10:36 says of Him, "He is Lord of all." The author of the epistle to the Hebrews said of Him, "He is the effulgence of His (God's) glory, and the very image (or 'exact expression') of his (God's) substance," and that He upholds all things by the Word of His power (Heb. 1:3). And Paul in Philippians 2:6 says that before He became man He existed originally "in the form of God." If the Bible makes anything as plain as day, it makes it plain as day that our Lord Jesus is a divine being with all the attributes, glory, majesty, and power that belong to God. He is God. Well then might the prophet Isaiah in his inspired vision of the coming of Jesus, cry, "His name shall be called Wonderful." If Jesus was not "very God of very God," then John was mistaken, and Paul was mistaken, and Jesus Himself was mistaken, and only that denomination that has never been noted for its prayerfulness, its spirituality, its devotion, its self-sacrifice, its missionary enterprise, that denomination which has only a history of building churches to see them die, that denomination alone is right, and John, Peter, Paul, and Jesus are wrong. Do you believe that? Can you believe that? No, a thousand times no. No man who is thoroughly sane in his head and thoroughly honest in his heart can believe that. Jesus then is a divine being. He is wonderful, most wonderful, wonderful beyond description, wonderful beyond conception. The wonderfulness of His being and nature will be the object of our glad and adoring contemplation and the theme of our highest praises throughout the endless eons that are to come, throughout eternity.

2. But there is another wonderful thing about the nature of Jesus. While He is divine He is at the same time a real man. "In the beginning was the Word, and the Word was with God, and the Word was God." But "the Word *became flesh* and dwelt among us." He was "the only begotten *Son of God*," but He is at the same time the *Son of man*. He is, Paul tells us in 1 Timothy 2:5, the "mediator between God and men, *Himself* man, Christ Jesus." Do you ask how are the perfect deity and the perfect humanity united in Jesus? I do not know. Neither do I know how spirit and body are united in myself, but I know that they are. I do not know how the divine nature that I received in the new birth is united with the physical and intellectual and moral nature that I received by my natural birth, but I know that it is, and so also I know that Jesus is perfectly divine and perfectly human. Well might the prophet say, "His name shall be called Wonderful."

II. Jesus Is Wonderful in His Character

But while Jesus is wonderful in His nature, in His divine glory and perfect humanity, He is not wonderful in His nature alone, He is wonderful in His character. His character was absolutely perfect. He was absolutely without blemish and without spot. He was not only faultless, but every possible perfection of character rested upon Him. There is not a perfection of character of which we can think that is not to be found in Him, and found in Him in its fullness. As the years go by and we study Him more and more carefully and come to see Him as He was and is more fully, the more the absolute perfection of His character shines forth. For thirty-four years He lived in a hostile world that sought to find some imperfection in Him, but they could find none. For eighteen centuries since, infidels have been hunting for some flaw in the character of Jesus, and they cannot find it. What would not the infidels give if they could only put their finger upon one single flaw, even one little defect in that character, but they cannot. Even the bitterest and boldest and most unscrupulous infidel of his day was forced to say, "I wish to say once for all that to that great and serene man I pay, I gladly pay, the homage of my admiration and my tears." Jesus in the perfection of His character is indeed wonderful. He is the wonder of the ages. He stands out absolutely peerless and alone. When any man ventures to put anyone else alongside of Jesus Christ, he at once loses the confidence of all candid and fair-minded men.

1. *Jesus was perfect in holiness.* Peter spoke of Him as "the holy One and the just" (Acts 3:14). John spoke of Him as "the Holy One" (1 John 2:20). Even the unclean spirits when they met Him were forced to cry out to Him, "I know thee, who thou art, the Holy One of God" (Mark 1:24). The epistle to the Hebrews speaks about Him as "holy, guileless, undefiled, separated from sinners." He passed through all our experiences of conflict and temptation yet "without sin" (Heb. 4:15). The dazzling white light that glorified the face and garments of Jesus on the Mount of Transfiguration was the out-shining of the moral purity within.

2. But He was not only perfect in holiness, *He was also perfect in love.* His love to God was perfect and so was His love to man. His love to God revealed itself in His unhesitating obedience to every com-mand of God, in His unreserved surrender to God's will, in His drawing back from no sacrifice that God demanded, in His delight in doing God's will, a delight so great that forgetting the long denied de-mands of bodily hunger, He could triumphantly say, "My meat is to do the will of Him who sent me and to accomplish His work" (John 4:34, RV). His love to God was absolutely perfect, but so was His love to man. His love to man took in all men, it took in the good, but it took in the vilest as well. It took in men like John and Nathaniel, but it took in also the demoniac of Gadara, the thief on the cross, the woman with the seven devils, and the woman who was taken in adul-tery. It took in His enemies for whom He prayed even as He endured the agonies and the reproaches and the shame they heaped upon Him, "Father, forgive them for they know not what they do." His love hes-itated at no sacrifice. "Though He was rich, yet for our sakes He be-came poor, that we through His poverty might become rich" (2 Cor. 8:9, RV). "Being in the form of God, He counted it not a thing to be grasped to be on an equality with God, but emptied Himself, taking the form of a servant, being made in the likeness of men; and being found in fashion as a man, He humbled Himself, becoming obedient unto death, yea, even the death of the cross" (Phil. 2:6–8). Wonderful, wonderful, wonderful love, that seeing full equality with God Him-self in honor and glory, turned His back upon all this and chose the

cow stable for His birthplace, the poor carpenter shop for His school, the contempt and rejection of men for His reward, the agony of Gethsemane and the shame and ignominy and torture of death upon the cross for its consummation, because by these things He could save the vile and worthless and outcast. Well might Isaiah say that Jesus' name should be called Wonderful. There are many other perfections in the character of Jesus, e.g., the perfection of His meekness and gentleness and humility and patience and courage, and manliness, but we cannot stop to dwell upon these now. Enough has been said to show that He is wonderful in character.

III. Jesus Is Wonderful in His Work

But as wonderful as Jesus is in His nature and in His character, He is not wonderful in His nature and character alone, He is also wonderful in His work.

1. In the first place *He made a perfect atonement for sin.* "All we like sheep have gone astray; we have turned every one to his own way; and the Lord hath laid on Him the iniquity of us all" (Is. 53:6). Every sin of ours was settled by the death of Jesus upon the cross. "Christ hath redeemed us from the curse of the law, having become a curse for us: for it is written, Cursed is every one that hangeth upon a tree" (Gal. 3:13). The death of Christ so perfectly atones for sin that the moment I believe in Jesus Christ and thus accept the atonement He has made for me, every sin of mine is blotted out from God's account and God reckons me as perfectly righteous in Him: "He who knew no sin He made to be sin in our behalf; that we might become the righteousness of God in Him" (2 Cor. 5:21). Is not this wonderful? Is it not amazing? that the vilest sinner there is in Los Angeles, or anywhere else on this earth, the liar, the thief, the blasphemer, the murderer, the harlot can come into this place tonight all crimson with the sins they have committed, and yet the death of Christ so perfectly atones for them all that the moment they accept that atonement all their sins are blotted out, and they become as white as snow. Oh, when the sins that I have committed come up before me, and they have been great (the sins of every one here tonight have been great), but when they come up I look away at the cross and I see Jesus hanging there, I hear His dying cry, "My God, my God, why hast thou

forsaken me?" and I hear His other cry, "It is finished," and I can see the Roman soldier draw back his spear, and I see it go crashing into that side. I see the life-blood pouring out, and I know that all my sins are atoned for. I know that,

> Jesus paid my debt,
>   All the debt I owe,
> Sin had left a crimson stain,
>   He washed it white as snow.

Oh, it is wonderful: the sin of the whole race atoned for at Calvary, and all that any man has to do to enjoy the fruits of that atonement is, just to accept it.

2. But Jesus not only made an atonement for sin, *He also saves from sin's power.* Jesus Christ has power to set any man who will put his trust in Him free from any sin, and the power of all sin. He Himself said, "If the Son shall make you free, ye shall be free indeed" (John 8:36). Is it not wonderful that there is not a man on earth today so completely in sin's power but that Jesus Christ can set him free? One night many years ago I met a man who had been a wanderer on the face of the earth for many years, but had come from a good family, had been well educated, had moved in good society, but who had turned his back on all this and had given himself up to a life of sin, and now at the age of perhaps 45 he was completely in sin's power. He was a large, powerful man, but he approached me with such hesitation and whispered in my ear the question, "Do you think Jesus Christ can save me?" I replied, "I know He can." Then I sat down and reasoned with Him out of the Scriptures, and He listened and believed and was saved. For years he was a happy Christian and enslaving sins were things of the past. Tonight he is with Christ in glory. That is but one case out of thousands and tens of thousands. I have known many, many such, personally. I have seen Jesus Christ set men free from sin in pretty much every state in the union. I have seen Him do it in England, Scotland, Ireland, Germany, France, Australia, New Zealand, Tasmania, China, Japan and India. There are right in this audience tonight many men and women whom Jesus has set free from an awful slavery that once held them captive. Indeed Jesus completely transforms men. The man who was once a blasphemer now prays. The man who once loved the vile book, now loves the Bible. The man who once told

questionable stories now sings hymns of praise. The men and women who once gave themselves over to sin and vice are now working for their fellowmen. "If any man is in Christ, He is a new creature; the old things are passed away; behold, they are become new" (2 Cor. 5:17). Oh, the work of Jesus is wonderful indeed, transforming demons into angels. One Sunday night I heard a man who a few years before was a ruffian, a drunken, profane, cruel brute, speaking to the best people of one of our eastern cities with great tenderness and pleading that they too accept the same Jesus who had so wonderfully transformed his life and that of his wife. Jesus is indeed wonderful in His work.

3. But *Jesus will do even more wonderful things in the future.* When He comes again, He will raise the dead with His voice, and we shall be caught up with them to meet Him in the air. He will transform us into His own perfect likeness. This old, weak, sickly, pain-racked body will be changed into the likeness of His own glorious body, free from every ache and pain, free from every weakness, free from every limitation, resplendent with a beauty never seen on earth, capable of unlimited activity. And He will transform us morally also, so that in our inmost character we shall be made just like Him. He will bring us fully into our glorious inheritance as heirs of God and joint-heirs with Himself, heirs of all God is and all God has, heirs of His wisdom, His power, His holiness. Oh, it is wonderful!

Jesus is indeed wonderful. He is wonderful in the infinite glory of His divine nature. He is wonderful in the matchless perfection of His character. He is wonderful in His work, blotting out all sin by His death, delivering from all sin by His resurrection life, transforming us from all remaining imperfection into the full glory of sons of God by His coming again. Jesus is the Wonderful One. Now what will you do with Him? What will you do with this wonderful Jesus? Will you accept Him or reject Him? Oh, the wisdom and the blessedness of those who accept Him. Oh, the folly and wretchedness of those who reject Him. What will you do tonight with this wonderful Jesus?

Study Questions

1. Why is Jesus wonderful in His nature?
2. Why is Jesus wonderful in His character?
3. Why is Jesus wonderful in His work?

6

The Fool's Creed

The fool hath said in his heart, there is no God (Ps. 14:1).

Our subject tonight is The Fool's Creed. Every intelligent man has a creed. You hear men in our days inveighing against creeds, but every man who thinks has a creed. A man's creed is what a man believes, and every man who thinks at all must believe something. The only man who believes nothing is the man whose mind is a perfect blank—the utter idiot. If any man says, "I believe nothing," he is either mistaken or deliberately lying. If he believes what he says to be true, when he says "I believe nothing," then he must at least believe that he believes nothing, and in that case he is, of course, mistaken when he says that he believes nothing. But if he is not mistaken when he says "I believe nothing," then it cannot be that he believes that he believes nothing, and in saying "I believe nothing," he is saying what he does not believe; in plain English, he is lying. To think is to believe, and the only man of whom it can be truly said he does not believe anything is the idiot. Our subject, however, tonight is not creeds in general, but a specific creed, The Fool's Creed. You will find a brief and plain statement of The Fool's Creed in Psalm 14:1, "The fool hath said in his heart, there is no God." The fool's creed has at least the merit of brevity, you can put it in two words, "no God." There is a great cry in our day for short creeds. The fool's creed ought to satisfy this demand. He has reduced his creed to two short words, to five letters, "no God." Why is the one who says in his heart "no God" a fool, or rather, why is he not merely a fool but "*the* fool," the fool of fools, the one consummate fool?

I. The Man Who Says There Is No God Is a Fool Because There Is a God

The first reason why the man who says there is no God is a fool is because there is a God. The proofs of the existence of a God, of an intelligent and beneficent creator and governor of the physical and moral universe are manifold and conclusive.

1. First of all, the observed facts of the physical universe point conclusively to the existence of an intelligent and beneficent creator and governor of that universe. There are four kingdoms in the universe as modern science investigates and knows it: (1) the inorganic kingdom, that is, the non-living world with its mechanical and chemical forces; (2) the vegetable kingdom; (3) the animal kingdom; (4) man. The inorganic kingdom is the least wonderful of all, yet how wonderful even it is in its vastness, in its conformity to law, in its structure and its operations, in the mechanical and chemical forces, ever working out such beneficent results. But when we come to the vegetable kingdom we take a great step upward into a kingdom whose unveiled mysteries fill the soul with increasing admiration and astonishment the more we explore them. The laws of nutrition, of growth and reproduction, how marvelous they are. Even the smallest of the plants, the plants that can be seen only with the aid of the microscope present models of symmetry, proportion and beauty that man can only try to imitate but cannot succeed in imitating. When we come to the animal kingdom we see superadded to the wonders of nutrition, growth and reproduction the still greater wonders of sensation and instinct. But take the last step upward to man, and we have superadded to these wonders the wonders of man's intellectual, moral and spiritual powers. Now all these things must be accounted for. We live in a wonderful world. The more we study it the more wonderful it appears, until it leads us on and out into the infinite, and until we see new meaning in the words of Psalm 19:1, "The heavens declare the glory of God; and the firmament showeth His handiwork," and in the words of Paul in Romans 1:20, "For the invisible things of Him [i.e., God] since the creation of the world are clearly seen, being perceived from the things that are made, even His everlasting power and divinity; that they may be without excuse." More and more as our knowledge enlarges do we find that everything has its use, even

down to the house fly, or the infusoria in the brook. Everything performs its functions according to law, from the sun 1, 283, 000 times as large as the earth and moving through space with incredible rapidity, down to the microscopic cilia of some simple form of life that sway lazily to and fro. Even the seeming monstrosities of nature are in accordance with law. It takes no profound knowledge of nature to see manifold adaptations to intelligent purpose. Take for example, the eye, the most marvelous camera obscura that was ever constructed, with its wonderful chemical and mechanical and sensory arrangement for vision, protection, and voluntary and involuntary use. Take the bird, with its hollow bones, its light feathers rendered waterproof by oil secretions. A scientific acquaintance with nature enlarges our view. The telescope can find no spaces so vast that order and law cease, nor can the microscope discover particles so small that they lack in symmetry, beauty and adaptation to their end. We live in a universe of law, beauty and utility. Now comes the question: how did this universe come to be as it is today? There are four possible suppositions about it:

(1) First, that it was always as it is now.

(2) Second, that it came to be as it is by chance, that the atoms that constitute the universe, in their eternal dance, have at last assumed their present associations and relations.

(3) Third, that there existed from all eternity certain material atoms containing in themselves the power of uniting and acting upon one another and developing into the present condition of the universe.

(4) Fourth, that the universe is the work of God.

This covers all the possible suppositions. Which is the true one? The first we know to be false. We know that the universe was not always as it is. The second is easily seen to be false. There is a chance that the atoms that constitute the universe in their eternal dance might assume the present associations and relations displayed in such marvelous orderliness, obedience to law, perfection of construction, and adaptation to intelligent ends. I say there may be a chance that is true, but while there is one chance that it might be so, there is an infinite number of chances against it. The bringing in of infinite ages in which it might happen does not help the theory, for while there might be one chance of our living in that particular age in which it did happen, there would be an infinite number of chances against it. Now the man who chooses to believe that in favor of which there is one chance, and against which there are an infinite number of chances can be justly characterized as in our text, "a fool." What would you call a man who believed that Webster's dictionary was not the intelligent product of a reasonable being, or a number of reasonable beings, but that the letters that constitute it were thrown down by chance and happened to fall into the shape we find them in the dictionary. There is only one word in the English language by which you would dream of characterizing such a man, you would call him a fool. But the theory that Webster's dictionary came to be in that way would not be a fractional part so foolish as the theory that the atoms that constitute this universe in their eternal dance at last assumed their present associations and relations displayed in such marvelous orderliness, obedience to law, and perfection of construction, and adaptation to intelligent ends, as we now find in the physical universe. The third theory, namely, that there existed from all eternity certain material atoms containing in themselves the power of uniting and acting upon one another and developing into the present condition of the universe, is untenable:

First, because if the atoms had existed from all eternity with the inherent power of combining into the present universe, they would have combined into it ages ago.

Second, because, while we have abundant experience of the construction of works exhibiting design by intelligent agents, we have absolutely no experience of unintelligent atoms having power of combining themselves into works exhibiting the marks of intelligence. Suppose one should attempt to throw a thousand dice and have them all turn up sixes, and succeed, what would you say? Every intelligent man would say the dice were loaded. But who loaded the dice of the universe? It is evident the third theory will not hold.

We have only the fourth theory remaining, namely, that the universe is the work of an intelligent and beneficent creator. There is a God. The theory of evolution does not in the least affect the argument. If the theory of evolution were true, it would only show the wonderful method by which this intelligent and beneficent creator worked out His plans.

2. Not only do the observed facts of the physical universe point conclusively to the existence of God, the facts of history point to the same thing. The hand of an intelligent, beneficent, just governor of the destinies of men is clearly seen in history, not only in Bible history but in all secular history as well. Anyone who carefully studies history will see that throughout the whole history of the race, as Coleridge puts it, "one increasing purpose runs." We see that above the human actors, kings, generals, statesmen, and commoners trying to carry out their own ambitions and purposes, there has been the guiding hand of One who has made even the wrath of men to praise Him, and who has worked out good from the lowest ambitions and vilest passions of men. Cities, kings, dynasties, and empires fall, but history marches right on to the goal that God has set for it—the kingdom of God on earth.

3. The Bible as it lies before us proves that there is a God. Here is a Book altogether unique to be accounted for. It must have an author. It is entirely different from any book, or all books, men have written it differs from them in its fulfilled prophecies, it differs from them in its indestructibility and invulnerability against all assaults; it differs from them in the purity and loftiness and comprehensiveness of its teachings; it differs from them in its power to save men and nations; it differs from them in its inexhaustible depths of wisdom and truth. This Book, to anyone who will study it deeply and thoroughly and candidly, is manifestly not man's book. Whose Book then is it? The more I study this Book the more overwhelmingly convinced I am that there must be a God back of it.

4. *Individual experience proves that there is a God.*

(1) Individual experience regarding answered prayer proves this. If I should go to a hole in the wall and order beefsteak rare, and beefsteak rare should be passed out, and then order mutton chops and mutton chops should be passed out, and some other time should order turkey and cranberry sauce, and turkey and cranberry sauce should be passed out, and if this should go on day after day, and what I ordered was passed out, I should certainly soon conclude that there was some intelligent person there attending to my orders, even though I saw no one. This is my exact experience with God. There have been many things that I have needed, that I have gone to God alone about and have told him of the need, and no human being knew of the need, and He has supplied the need, supplied it oftentimes in such a way that the

connection between the prayer and the thing obtained was of such a character that it was clear that the prayer brought the gift. There have been times in my life when I have risked everything that men hold dear upon there being a God who answered prayer on the conditions laid down in the Bible. I have staked my health and that of my family, my temporal needs, my reputation, everything that men hold dear for time and eternity, on God's answering prayer on the conditions laid down in the Bible, and I have won. For sixty years George Mueller housed and fed orphans by the thousand and secured the supplies for the work entirely by prayer. No one was ever told of the need, no one but God, and not one penny of debt was ever incurred; and money and supplies came, oftentimes came only at the last moment, sometimes came when it would seem impossible that they should come on time, but there was never a day nor a meal in which God failed to answer prayer.

(2) Individual experience in regard to salvation proves that there is a God. Lost men, men utterly lost, men with whom every human effort to save has failed, have at last cast themselves upon God, the God of the Bible, the God who could only be approached through Jesus Christ, God in Christ, and have found salvation, such a salvation as God alone could work. They have been recreated, made new creatures, they have been raised from the dead.

The man who in anything proceeds upon the supposition that there is a God, just such a God as the Bible pictures, will always find this supposition works well in practice. To sum up thus far, the observed facts of the physical universe, the facts of history, the absolutely unique undeniable character of the Bible, and individual experience all prove to a demonstration that there is a God. Therefore, he that says "no God" is a fool.

II. The Man Who Says There Is No God Is a Fool Because Not Only Is There a God, but It Is Well That There Is

In the second place, the man who says in his heart that there is no God is a fool, not only because there is a God but also because it is well that there is a God. Please notice that it is *"in his heart"* that the fool says, "no God"; that is, he denies the existence of God because he does not wish to believe that there is a God. For a man to wish that there were no God shows him to be a fool because there not only is a God, but *it is well that there is,* and to wish that there were not is a mark of consummate folly. If there is a God, a God such as the Bible describes, the present life and the future life is full of brightness and hope to anyone who will take the right attitude toward that God; but if there is no God, then the sun has gone out of the heavens and a darkness that can be felt broods over the universe. If there is no God we know nothing of what is in store for us, the present apparent harmony and orderliness of the universe may cease any moment, and all plunge into chaos. If there is no God, history has no guiding hand and no certain destiny. If there is no God, reason and thought, conscience and right, purity and love have no certain and eternal basis. If there is no God, we have no security for a moment that blind fate that rules all may not seize, and rend and crush us and plunge us into dark, unutterable, eternal misery. This is a true picture of our position in the universe if there is no God. What intelligent man would wish to live in a universe without a God? Surely it is the fool, the fool of fools, the consummate fool of the ages, who says in his heart, "no God."

There are many who do not say with their lips, "no God," but who say it in their "heart." They are not theoretical atheists, but they are practical atheists. Anyone who does not surrender his will to God is a practical atheist. Anyone in this building tonight who has not surrendered to God is practically saying in his heart, "there is no God," and is, therefore, a fool. To sum up there is a God. Thank God that there is. There is just such a God as the Bible reveals. There is then but one right thing, but one wise thing for any man here tonight to do, that is surrender to His will. The only path of wisdom in the face of the proven facts, is to give ourselves in utter obedience to Him, and to accept as our mediator Him whom God has set forth to be the mediator between us and Himself, accept Him whom He has provided to be a sin-bearer, as our sin-bearer, accept Him whom He has exalted to be both Lord and King, as our Lord and King tonight. Who will do it? Who will do it now?

Study Questions

1. What does it mean to say "Every man has a creed"?
2. What is "the Fools Creed" from Psalm 14:1?

7

No Hope

Ye were at that time separated from Christ, alienated from the commonwealth of Israel, and strangers from the covenants of the promise, having no hope and without God in the world (Eph. 2:12).

These words describe the appalling condition of the Ephesians before they were saved, but tonight I wish to impress upon you just three words in this dark picture, "having no hope." There are no words in the language more dreadful than those two words, "no hope." A doctor stands beside a bed upon which lies a man who is very ill. The doctor's finger is upon the sick man's pulse; he is looking intently into the sick man's eyes; he is eagerly watching every movement and the way in which the sick man breathes. The sick man's wife and children are gathered around the bed, looking anxiously first at the husband and father, and then at the doctor. At last the doctor looks up and says, "no hope." A ship has sprung a leak in mid-ocean; the sailors are working with all their might at the pumps; the water from hold dashes across the deck into the ocean. An officer stands by, now and then dropping a line into the hold measuring the depth of the water, seeking to learn if it is falling or increasing. At last he looks up and cries, "It is no use, boys; there is no hope." A man has been making every effort to keep off financial ruin, but at last he is obliged to throw up his hands in despair and cry out, "No hope." A little company of men are defending a citadel against a yelling horde of murderous, bloodthirsty Turks without. Gathered in the citadel are not only the men who are defending it, but a company of women and children. The men know well that if they surrender it means death to them and worse than death to the women and children, and bravely they fight on to defend the citadel, but now their last round of ammunition is exhausted; there is a crash as the doors give way below, and a cry rings through the citadel, "No hope, no hope!" Ah, those are dark words, but they are even darker yet in import in the connection in which we find them in our text. Better to be without anything else than to be without hope. We may be in great present distress, but if we have a good hope for the future, it matters little. We may have great present prosperity, but if we have no good hope for the future, it is of little worth. I would rather be the poorest man who walks the streets of this city tonight and have a good hope for the future, than to be the richest millionaire and have no hope for the future.

I. Who Have No Hope?

There are three classes who have no hope. But what do we mean by hope? Desire, no matter how strong it may be, is not hope. Mere expectation, no matter how confident it may be, is not hope. We use the word hope in a very careless way in much of our modern speech, but in the Bible the word is used with great care. Hope is a *well-founded expectation for the future*. Any expectation that has not a sure foundation is not really hope.

1. *First of all the man who denies or doubts the existence of a personal God, a wise, mighty, loving ruler of the universe, has no hope.* He may cherish fond wishes about the future; he may even entertain confident expectations about it, but wishes are not hope, and expectations, no matter how confident, are not hope. His expectations are not well founded; and therefore, they are not hope. The man who denies or doubts that a wise, mighty and loving Father presides over his destiny and that of others, can have no well-founded expectations for the future. If he has what he calls a hope, it is utterly irrational and baseless. If there is not a God who is wise enough to know what is best, and loving enough to desire what is best, and powerful enough to carry out what is best, if there is not such a God as that, there is absolutely no guarantee that at any moment nature may not plunge into chaos and human history into pandemonium, absolutely no guarantee that both nature and man may not be involved any day in a universal sway of pain, destruction and despair; no guarantee that both nature and

society may not become hell. Man's only rational foundation for hope in the future is the existence of an intelligent, beneficent, and omnipotent God ruling nature and the affairs of men. Atheism and agnosticism are unspeakably dark faiths if any man has the courage to think them out to their logical conclusion; most atheists and agnostics dare not do it. But some agnostics and atheists have done it. Listen to the words of two men men who were agnostics and who have thought through their creed of unbelief toward its logical and utterly dark conclusion. First of all listen to the words of David Strauss, who began by questioning the miraculous and by trying to reconstruct the life of the Lord Jesus from the Gospel material, eliminating the supernatural and having the character and conduct left, but who wound up in blank agnosticism. He says:

In the enormous machine of the universe, amid the whirl and hiss of its jagged iron wheels, amid the deafening crash of its ponderous stamps and hammers, in the midst of this whole terrific commotion, man finds himself placed with no security, for a moment, that on an imprudent motion a wheel may not seize and rend him, or a hammer crush him to powder.

That is an awful picture, but if there is no personal God, no God wise enough to know what is best, loving enough to desire what is best, and powerful enough to carry out what is best, no such God as the Bible presents, then Strauss's conclusion is inevitable, only he has understated rather than overstated the darkness of the outlook. Now listen to another, Morley: "The millions of hewers of wood and drawers of water, come upon the earth that greets them with no smile, stagger blindly under dull burdens for a season, and are then shoveled silently back under the ground with no outlook and no hope." Pretty dark is it not this creed of agnosticism? But if there is no God these statements, terrible as they are, appalling as they are, full of utter despair as they are, are understatements of the hopelessness and blackness of the outlook. One night some years ago the thought came to me, suppose that instead of the God of wisdom and love in whom we believe, there sat upon the throne of this universe a malignant being, a being just the opposite of the God of the Bible, what then? and I began to think it out until my brain almost reeled. The denier or the doubter of the existence of an omniscient, omnipotent, loving God, has no hope, no rational, well-founded expectation for the future, a very dark hell may be his portion any moment. No wonder the inspired Psalmist calls the one who says in his heart there is no God a fool (Ps. 14:1).

2. *The man who denies the truth of the Bible has no hope.* It does not necessarily follow because a man denies the truth of the Bible that he does not believe in the existence of God. A man may believe in God, he may be a theist, and yet not believe the Bible. But even though a man is a believer in God, if he rejects the Bible he has no hope, that is, he has no expectation for the future that has a solid and certain foundation underneath it. The conception that one gets of God from mere philosophy and pure reasoning is altogether too inadequate to form a rational foundation for an intelligent hope. Furthermore, the God of philosophy is necessarily an ever vanishing quantity, for philosophy is always in a flux. Philosophy never reaches conclusions that are final and settled. I once was very fond of the study of philosophy; I waded through the teachings of the great philosophers from the time of Socrates down to the time of the modern German philosophers. It seemed a fascinating study. At times I thought I had reached settled conclusions, but at last I discovered what every other thoughtful student of philosophy discovers sooner or later, that one philosopher comes upon the scene to demolish all who have gone before him, only in turn to have his own conclusions demolished by those who follow him. The only conception of God that gives a man a good basis for expectation for the life that now is, or the life which is to come, is the conception of God found in the Bible. It is true many who reject the Bible borrow their idea of God from the Bible and build up a superstructure of hope upon the conception of God which they have borrowed from the Bible, and then fancy they have reasoned it out, and then they go on to discredit the Bible and throw it away; but by so doing unwittingly they tear out the very foundation of their own faith. If you give up the Bible you most logically give up the contents of the Bible, the teachings of the Bible—and if you give up the teachings of the Bible you must give up hope. There is no hope for the man who discards the Bible; that is, no well-founded expectation for the future. Discard the Bible, discredit the Bible, and the future is dark and full of possibilities of evil, awful possibilities of evil.

3. *The man who believes in the Bible but does not accept and confess the Christ the Bible presents as his own personal Savior and Master, has*

no hope. Many a man fancies he has a ground for hope because he is not an infidel or an atheist. Many a man says to me, "Why, I believe the Bible, sir," but that is not the whole question. Have you accepted the Christ of the Bible as your own personal Savior, and are you confessing Him before the world as your Lord, and are you proving that to be an honest confession by doing as He says? The Bible holds out absolutely no hope to any except those who accept the Savior whom it is its main purpose to reveal. In this Bible which you profess to believe we read in John 3:36, "He that believeth on the Son hath everlasting life; and he that believeth not the Son *shall not see life; but the wrath of God abideth on him.*" Again we read in this Bible which you profess to believe, in 2 Thessalonians 1:7–9, "The Lord Jesus shall be revealed from heaven with the angels of His power in flaming fire, rendering vengeance to them that know not God, and *that obey not the gospel of our Lord Jesus Christ; who shall suffer everlasting destruction from the face of the Lord* and from the glory of His might." And still further we read in this Bible which you profess to believe, "If we sin willfully after we have received the knowledge of the truth, there remaineth no more sacrifice for sins, but a certain fearful looking for of judgment and fiery indignation, which shall devour the adversaries. He that despised Moses' law died without mercy under two or three witnesses; of how much sorer punishment, suppose ye, shall he be thought worthy, who hath trodden underfoot the Son of God (and that is what you are doing if you have not accepted Him as your Savior and confessed Him as your Lord), and hath counted the blood of the covenant, wherewith he was sanctified, a common thing, and hath insulted the Spirit of grace?" (Heb. 10:26–29). The one who believes the Bible but rejects the Savior whom the Bible presents, has every vestige of hope swept away by that very Book he believes. The man who believes the Bible but rejects the Christ of the Bible has no hope, the future has in it nothing but the appalling blackness of utter despair.

II. In What Sense Have These Three Classes No Hope?

We see, then, that the atheist and the agnostic have no hope, that the infidel and skeptic have no hope, that the orthodox believer in the Bible who rejects Christ as a personal Savior and Lord has no hope. In what sense have they no hope?

1. *They have no hope for the life that now is,* no well-founded and sure expectation of blessedness for the life that now is (1) *In the first place, they have no guarantee of continued prosperity.* They may be very prosperous today, they may have perfect health, a comfortable income, hosts of friends, every earthly thing that the heart would desire, but unless they are right with God, unless they have accepted His Son Jesus Christ and therefore have a right to claim the promises of the Bible as their own, there is absolutely no guarantee that these things which they now possess will continue to be theirs twenty-four hours. A thousand things may occur to change it all. Upheavals of nature may come, such as laid San Francisco in ruins a few years ago, wrecking the fortunes of thousands and bringing bereavement to many homes; social upheavals may come, political catastrophes may come, war may come; indeed the black portent of war overhangs every people on earth today. This country by its recent election may have expressed its unwillingness to go to war, but that will not necessarily keep us out of war. What may other countries plan regarding us? Innumerable other diverse occurrences may come. A thoughtful man can conceive of many things that might occur that would sweep away in a few minutes the vast fortunes of even a Rockefeller or a Morgan. Indeed, I am strongly inclined to believe that it is almost certain that all these fortunes will be swept away in the next ten or twenty years as an outside limit, either by great social and political revolutions, or by the coming of the Lord Jesus Christ. (2) *In the next place they have no guarantee of continued capacity to enjoy prosperity, even if it continues.* A man's prosperity may continue and he lose all capacity to enjoy it. When I lived in Chicago, one of its wealthiest men had been for several years in a madhouse. His business continued to prosper, prosper enormously, but what good did that fact do him? He had no capacity to enjoy what he possessed. No man out of Christ has any guarantee of continued capacity to enjoy the things of the life that now is. He may have the money to spread his table with all the delicacies that a gourmand might desire, but if he has dyspepsia what good will it do him? No, the man out of Christ has no hope, no well-founded expectation, for the life that now is. (3) Furthermore, *the man out of Christ has no guarantee of continued life.* There is never but a step between any man and death. Every step that each one of us takes each day is but a march toward the grave. Every step we take is along the

edge of the grave, and any moment the edge may crumble away and we fall into the grave. It takes but one little snip of the shears of fate to sever the cord of life. Of course, if a man is a true Christian, this fact has no terrors for him; for what men call death is simply departing to be with Christ, "which is very far better." No man out of Christ has a good hope for the next ten minutes. Let us go back some years and go to New York City. We stand in the doorway of the library of the richest American of his day. His property inventories at 196,000,000 dollars. He is in close conversation with a business friend; they are discussing how to make that 196, 000, 000 a little more. Ah, you say, as you look on that multimillionaire, he has bright hopes for many years to come. You are absolutely mistaken; no hope, absolutely no hope, for ten minutes; even as you look at him he pitches forward from the chair to the floor, and when Mr. Garrett picks William H. Vanderbilt from the floor he is a corpse. How much is he worth now? The next day one man asked another on 'change in New York, "how much did William H. Vanderbilt leave?" The other man replied, "He left it all." Yes, he left it all. Men out of Christ have "no hope" for the life that now is.

2. *But infinitely worse than this is the fact that they have no hope for the life that is to come.* This earthly life is but a brief span at the very longest. Earthly life when I was a boy appeared very long to me, but the other day I was reading some words that I wrote about twenty years ago. I said, "Life used to appear long when I was a boy, but now that I have just passed the fortieth milestone and feel confident my race is more than half run, it seems very short, very short." But now that twenty years more have passed, it seems shorter still. It seems shorter every year. I never knew time to fly as it has the past month. We are hurrying on toward the grave and eternity faster than the automobiles yesterday whirled around the course in the Vanderbilt Cup Race. Do you realize, men and women, that in thirty years you will be in heaven or hell? Yes, some of you in twenty years, some of you in five years? Do you realize that some of you who are here tonight will be in heaven or hell within a year? But ETERNITY IS LONG; how it stretches out. Let us stand now and look out down through the stretches of eternity, look yonder, a thousand years have passed, are we any nearer the end of eternity? No. A million years have passed and still it stretches on before us; a billion, a trillion, a quadrillion, a vingintillion, are we

any nearer the end? Ah, no! On and on and on! The farther we look ahead the longer it stretches out. It is an awful thing to have no hope for eternity. (1) *The man out of Christ has no hope of blessedness after death.* No, there is no light in the grave for the Christless man. Let us stand and look into the Christless man's grave right now. What do you see? Oh, it is dark and cold. Black, black, black, eternal blackness, eternal despair. (2) *There is no hope of glad reunion with friends who have gone or who may go.* The believer loses his friends, but he does not sorrow as those who have no hope (1 Thess. 4:13), he knows that the time is fast hurrying on when the Lord Himself shall descend from heaven with a shout, with the voice of the archangel, and with the trump of God; and when the bodies of his loved ones who have gone before shall be raised, and when he "shall be caught up *together with them* to meet the Lord in the air," and so shall they ever be with the Lord and with one another (1 Thess. 4:14–16). Ah, Christless man, you will never meet that sainted mother again. What a noble woman she was, what a dark hour it was when she left you to depart and be with Christ. How you have longed for a reunion with that woman who, as you thought, was the noblest woman that ever lived on earth. But you will never meet again. Ah, Christless woman, you will never meet again that sweet and innocent babe who has departed to be with Christ. When God put that babe in your arms, how you hugged it to your breast; how as the days went by you looked down into those eyes so full of mystery and meaning; but the day came when God in His infinite wisdom took that child from this world, and now it is safe in the arms of Jesus, but you are out of Christ, and you will never depart to be with Christ. You will never meet that sweet babe again. Oh, Christless husband, how dear and noble was that woman who for some years walked by your side, and then she was called away, and now she is with Christ in glory, but you will never meet her again. No, there is no hope for the man out of Christ of happy reunions in that world where there is no sorrow, no pain, no sickness, no death, no separation.

3. *For the man out of Christ there is not hope of pardon in the eternal world.* Pardon is freely offered *here* to anyone who will accept Christ, but there is no pardon beyond the grave. Our Lord Himself has told us that those who die in their sins, where He goes they cannot come (John 8:21). There is no hope of escaping from the wrath of God

against the sin of unbelief. "The wages of sin is death. The gift of God is eternal life," but that life is "in Jesus Christ our Lord," and if you reject Him and die without Him there is no hope. "He that believeth on the Son hath everlasting life, but he that believeth not the Son, shall not see life, but the wrath of God abideth upon him." No, there is no hope of escaping the wrath of God against sin and unbelief, if one goes out of this world without Christ.

"No hope," "no hope," "no hope," for the man out of Christ, no hope for the life that now is, no hope for the life to come, no hope for time, no hope for eternity. There is nothing ahead but the blackness of darkness. The joys of the present may last a few days, but even that is not certain, but it is certain that they cannot last long, and then nothing left but separation from God with all its consequent misery and degradation for all eternity.

III. The Believer in Christ Has Hope

Before we close let it be said that the believer in Christ has hope.

1. *He has hope for the life that now is.* It is true that he does not know what the future may bring, but he has the sure Word of God for it that it will bring nothing but good, he knows that all things work together for good for those that love God (Rom. 8:28). He knows that he needs to "be careful for nothing, but in everything by prayer and supplication with thanksgiving, [make his] requests known unto God," and that "the peace of God which passeth all understanding, shall keep [his mind and heart] in Christ Jesus. He knows that "God will supply [his every need] according to His riches in glory, in Christ Jesus" (Phil. 4:6, 7, 19). He knows that "God spared not His only begotten Son but freely gave Him for" him, and by that guarantee he knows that He will withhold no good thing from him, that with Him He will freely give him all things (Rom. 8:32).

2. *The Christian has hope for the life to come; he has "hope of eternal life which God who cannot lie hath promised"* (Titus 1:2). How certain that hope, resting upon the Word of God who cannot lie; how magnificent that hope, eternal life. He has in the world to come "an inheritance incorruptible and undefiled, and that fadeth not away, reserved in heaven for" him (1 Pet. 1:4). He has the assurance of the Word of God and the indwelling Spirit of God that he is a child of

God, and if a child, then an heir, an heir of God and a joint heir with Jesus Christ, and that any "sufferings of this present time are not worthy to be compared with the glory which shall be revealed in" Him (Rom. 8:16). Wonderful hope, immeasurable hope, glorious hope of the Christian, but the man out of Christ has "no hope."

Friends, which do you prefer tonight, the no hope of a man out of Christ, or the glorious hope of the one who has received Christ as his Savior, surrendered to Him as his Lord and Master, and confessed Him as such before the world? You have your choice. Every one here has his choice. Which will you take? All of us here tonight are like men standing on the seashore and looking out over the boundless ocean of eternity. Toward some of us, toward every one of us here tonight who is a true Christian, there come gallant vessels loaded with gold and silver and precious stones, with every sail set, wafted swiftly toward us by the breezes of God's favor. But toward those of us who have rejected Him or neglected Him, those of us who have never publicly confessed Him before the world, there come no vessels, but dismantled wrecks, with no cargoes but the *livid corpses* of lost opportunities, over which hover the vultures of eternal despair, driven on toward us with mad velocity before the fast rising tempest of the wrath and indignation of an all holy and almighty God. Glorious hope, and no hope, which will you take?

Study Questions

1. Who has "no hope"?
2. What is the definition of hope?
3. In what ways does the believer in Christ have hope?

8

Where Will You Spend Eternity?

Where goest thou? (John 16:5).

Our subject tonight is, Where Will You Spend Eternity? You will find the text in John 16:5, "Where goest thou?" Jesus Christ was about to leave this world. He told the disciples that he was going, but none of them asked Him where He was going. He reproved them for not asking. Well He might, for the most important question that can face any man when he comes to leave this present world is "Where goest thou?" or "Where will you spend eternity?" A friend of mine was in a store one evening and an elderly man came in and said to the proprietor as he bought a cigar, "Dr. Torrey is going to preach tomorrow night on 'Where will you spend eternity?' " It had been an exceedingly cold winter, and the proprietor replied, "Some of the poor people around here recently have felt as though they would like to spend it in some place where it was hot." I suppose the man was simply thoughtless when he said it, but it marks a shallow man, a very shallow man, to be thoughtless on a question like this. It will not do to dismiss a question like this in that way. Some of you would like to dismiss it in some such light, thoughtless way. You will play the fool if you do. When Harry Hayward, the brutal Minneapolis murderer, who murdered a woman who had been kind to him in order to get a few dollars from her, stood upon the gallows and the drop was about to fall, he made a funny speech and at the last jestingly twitched the rope about his neck and said to the sheriff, "Let her go, I stand pat." I fancy he thought he was smart. No intelligent man thought so. They set him down as a fool and a brute. And so, my friends, you who are disposed to joke about this solemn question we have before us tonight, I beg of you do not do it. Your friend out of courtesy, may laugh at your joke, but in his inmost heart he will think you a fool, and in your inmost heart you will know he is right. That then is our subject tonight, "Where goest thou?" or "Where will you spend eternity?"

I. First of All, Remember That There Is an Eternity

That is certain. We may try to shut our eyes to the fact, but the fact stands. Look ahead tonight. You may live five years, ten years, twenty years, thirty, forty, fifty years. But then what? The fifty years will soon be gone. Then what? ETERNITY! On it stretches before us, on and on and on. Never ending centuries will roll on, ages roll on, but still eternity stretches on and on. It will ever stretch on, never any nearer an end. Oh, thank God for eternity. If I knew I were to live a thousand years, it would not satisfy me. If I were to live a million years, it would not satisfy me. I would always be thinking of the end that would come some time. I am glad that as I look out into the future I see an eternity that has absolutely no end. There is an eternity.

II. In the Second Place, Remember You Must Spend That Eternity Somewhere

The time will never come when you cease to be, the time will never come when you pass into nowhere. You will be somewhere throughout all eternity. Men sometimes try to believe that when they die they will cease to be. A friend of mine once told me that was what he believed; that when he died that would be the end of him. He was very sure of it. Not long after his mother died, and he wrote me a letter about her having passed into a better life. His atheistic philosophy would not stand. Men who live like beasts naturally wish to believe that they will die like beasts, but there is something in all our souls that tells us that it is not so. It is your *beastly* self that says that death ends all. Your better self denies it. But, however that may be, there is One who came to us out of eternity, came to us from the unseen, eternal world, came to us from God, with whom He had been through all eternity. He presented His perfectly satisfactory credentials of His divine origin, of His having come from eternity, Jesus

Christ, and He has told us that there is an eternity for each of us and that we must spend it somewhere.

III. Remember in the Third Place That the Question As to Where You Will Spend Eternity Is Vastly More Important Than the Question As to Where You Will Spend Your Present Life

How anxious we are about where we shall spend our present life. Shall I spend my life in a cottage or in a palace? Shall I spend my life in the midst of the luxuries of wealth or amid the privations of poverty? Shall I spend my life in the midst of congenial companions or amid bitter foes? Shall I spend my present life in health and happiness or in pain and weariness and sorrow? How anxious we are about these questions. But they are of comparatively no importance. Suppose I spend my life in a palace. Suppose that I have all that money can buy. I dress elegantly and fare sumptuously every day. I go to parties and often off to Florida, the Sandwich Islands or Europe. Oh, what a happy life! Not very. But suppose it is. How long will it last? Ten years, twenty years, forty years, fifty years, and it is all over. What then? *What then?* The coffin, the grave, eternity. On the other hand, suppose I spend my life in poverty. I have little cooped-up rooms, not very clean. I have very poor food, and perhaps oftentimes not enough of that. I wear shabby clothes. I have to work hard for very small pay. The rich brush by me and my children in the street, and think us of little more account than the dogs and cats. Oh, what a wretched life! Not necessarily. It may be a very happy life. Ten years, twenty years, forty years, and it is all over. And what then? Eternity! An eternity of joy, or it may be an eternity of woe, to which any wretchedness I knew here is as nothing, nothing at all. Ah, the question of where we shall spend eternity is the important question. Suppose I am taking a day's journey to a place where I shall spend forty years. Which is the more important, the accommodations I shall have on the cars or the accommodations I shall have when I get there? This life is a day's journey to an endless eternity. Some travel the journey in a common day coach, a poor one at that, but they travel to a mansion to which the stateliest palace on earth is as nothing. We can easily put up with some inconveniences by the way. Some travel in a very sumptuous Pullman palace car, or on a deluxe train, but they are traveling to a hovel, poor, loathsome, pestilential, nay, they are traveling to a prison-house, to a dungeon, nay they are traveling to hell itself, where they shall spend eternity. I don't envy them. Take the multimillionaires who are traveling at express speed to hell. Do you envy them? I don't. Poor wretches! This question of where we shall spend eternity is a far more important question than the question of the comforts we shall enjoy by the way. Are you giving this question the consideration its importance demands? Many of you will soon be there. The brother of a friend of mine lay near death, near eternity's door. He had been a professed Christian in early life, but he had become a backslider, and very bitter. He would not allow anyone to speak to him about Christ or the future. His wife and daughters and mother were praying constantly. They could not let him die thus. His brother was praying. At last he could keep silence no longer. He said "Willie, when you used to go off on a journey did you make preparations for it?" He looked up with surprise, "Why, certainly." "Willie, do you know you are about to take a long journey? Have you made any preparations?" "No, none." "Don't you think you ought?" "It's no use. Jesus won't take me now, I am too great a sinner." His brother quoted to him the wonderful promises to sinners found in this Book, and he found peace at last. But what if he had gone to that great eternity persistently refusing to make preparations? Men and women, young men and young women, don't be foolish. Face this great question, "Where shall I spend eternity?"

IV. The Next Point to Consider Is That It Is Possible for Us to Know Where We Shall Spend Eternity

Some think it is all guesswork. It is with some. It need not be. Jesus knew where He would spend eternity. He said, "I go to Him that sent me." Paul knew where he would spend eternity. He said, "For me to die is gain." And again, "I depart to be with Christ which is very far better" (Phil. 1:23). And still again,

I have fought the good fight, I have finished the course, I have kept the faith; henceforth there is laid up for me a crown of righteousness which the Lord, the righteous judge, shall give me at that day: and not only to me but also to all them that have loved His appearing (2 Tim. 4:7, 8).

Albert Cookman knew where he would spend eternity. As he was dying, he lifted up his voice and shouted, "I am sweeping through the gates to the New Jerusalem." D. L. Moody knew where he would spend eternity. As he was slipping away from life he said, "This is my coronation day, I have long been looking forward to it." I know where I shall spend eternity. "How do you know?" someone will ask. I have the sure word of God for it. You can anyone of you know if you will. Now you men who call yourselves agnostics, skeptics, and infidels and Universalists and Unitarians and Spiritualists, and Christian Scientists and theosophists, do you *know* where you will spend eternity? Do you *really know?* Be honest with yourselves now. You cannot afford to be deceived, do you know? No, no, no, you don't know. Well I do know.

V. The Fifth Fact to Bear in Mind Is That We Will Spend Eternity in One of Two Places—in Heaven or in Hell

The exact location of heaven and the exact location of hell is not a question we need to enter into. The character of the places is the important question. Heaven is a place of holiness, happiness and love. Hell is a place of violence, misery and hate. In one or the other you and I shall spend eternity. With Christ or with the devil. With the holy and pure or with the profane, the blasphemous, the vile. Which will it be for all eternity?

VI. Now Let Me Pin into Your Memory Another Thought, Where You Will Spend Eternity Will Be Settled in the Life That Now Is

Jesus Christ says in John 8:24, "I said therefore unto you, that ye shall die in your sins. For if ye believe not that I am He, ye shall die in your sins." And we read in the twenty-first verse of the same chapter, "Then said Jesus again unto them, I go my way, and ye shall seek me, and shall die in your sins, Where I go, ye cannot come." In other words Jesus says that unless we believe in Him we shall die in our sins, and that if we do die in our sins, our eternal destiny is sealed. Again the apostle Paul says in 2 Corinthians 5:10, "We must all appear before the judgment seat of Christ, that every one may receive *the things done in his body,* according to that he hath done, whether it be good or bad." This makes it clear that where we will spend eternity is decided by the deeds done in the body, the things done this side the grave. It makes it clear that where we will spend eternity will be settled in the life that now is. Now many people do not like to believe that. They know that their present life is a very poor preparation for eternity, so they don't like to think that their present life settles their eternal destiny. But it does. Jesus taught that plainly enough when He said as quoted above: "If ye believe not that I am He, ye shall die in your sins, Where I go ye cannot come." Schemes of future probation are pure speculations with absolutely no foundation in fact and contrary to the plain teaching of the Book that never lies. It is not a question, friends, of what we would like to believe, but what is true. But some man rises and says, "I don't think that where we shall spend eternity is settled in this life. I think men will have another chance." I reply, "It doesn't make a particle of difference what you think, or what I think. The question is what does God say." But you still persist in saying, "But some very scholarly men and some very brilliant men like Lyman Abbott, for example, think there is to be another chance." I reply, "Who is Lyman Abbott? A man who some eighty years or so ago came out of the great unknown, grew to manhood, talked a good deal, said some wise things and, as everyone knows, a good many foolish things, and in five years or less he will disappear again and soon be forgotten." But who is Jesus? One who was in the beginning, was with God and was God. Some eighteen centuries ago He took upon Himself a human form, lived thirty odd years on this planet, spake as never a man spake before nor since, revealing the truths He had learned in eternal fellowship with God, was killed by those of His time for claiming to be the Son of God, was raised from the dead by God Himself in testimony that His claim was true, was exalted to God's right hand "far above all rule and authority and power and dominion and every name that is named in this world or in the world to come." Which are you going to believe Lyman Abbott or Jesus Christ. Pastor Russell or Jesus Christ? If you have any sense you will believe Jesus Christ. Through all the centuries of Christian history men have appeared who have differed with Jesus Christ, men who have been accounted just as scholarly and brilliant by their generations as these men who today presume to set up their opinions against the teachings of Jesus Christ, and they have disappeared from the stage again and their vaunted discoveries have not stood the test of time; but the teachings of Jesus Christ have stood the test of nearly nineteen centuries. It ought not to take a man of fair average common sense very long to decide whom to believe under such circumstances. Believe Jesus Christ. Well, if you do believe Jesus Christ, write it down that where we shall spend eternity is settled in this life, settled this side of the grave.

VII. Just One Point More, Where You Spend Eternity Will Be Determined by What You Do with Jesus Christ

If you accept Jesus Christ as your Lord and Savior, you will spend eternity with Him. If you reject Jesus Christ, you will spend eternity away from Him. Listen to the sure word of God. "He that believeth on the Son hath everlasting life: and he that believeth not the Son shall not see life; but the wrath of God abideth on Him" (John 3:36). Listen again. "The Lord Jesus shall be revealed from heaven with His mighty angels, in flaming fire, rendering vengeance to them that know not God, and to them that obey not the Gospel of our Lord Jesus Christ: who shall suffer punishment even everlasting destruction from the face of the Lord and from the glory of His might" (2 Thess. 1:7–9, see RV). Where we spend eternity will be determined by what we do with Jesus Christ in the life that now is.

Let us sum up what we have seen tonight. First there is an eternity; second, we must spend that eternity somewhere; third, the question where you will spend eternity is vastly more important than the question of where you will spend your present life; fourth, it is possible for us to know where we shall spend eternity; fifth, we shall spend eternity in one of two places, in heaven or in hell; sixth, where we spend eternity will be settled in the life that now is; seventh, where you spend eternity will be determined by what you do with Jesus Christ. My friend, where goest thou? Where will you spend eternity? There is a story that has been often told but that I wish to repeat tonight. In 1867 a young French nobleman went to London to consult Dr. Forbes Winslow, the eminent pathologist in diseases of the mind. He took letters of introduction from eminent men in France, among others one from Napoleon III, who was then Emperor of France. Reaching London he called upon Dr. Forbes Winslow and presented his letters of introduction. Having read them Dr. Winslow asked him what was the trouble. The young man replied, "I cannot sleep. I have not had a good night's sleep for two years, and unless I get sleep I will go insane." Dr. Forbes Winslow asked him why he could not sleep. He replied he could not tell. "Have you lost money?" "No." "Have you suffered in honor or reputation?" "Not that I know of." "Have you lost friends?" "Not recently." "Why then can you not sleep?" The young man replied that he would rather not tell. Dr. Winslow said, "Unless you tell me I cannot help you." "Well then if you must know, I am an infidel. My father was an infidel before me, but strange as it may appear to you, though I am an infidel and though my father was an infidel before me, when I go to bed at night I am haunted with this thought: Eternity, and where shall I spend it? And it drives all sleep from me. It haunts me the whole night through. If I succeed in getting a little sleep my sleeping thoughts are worse than my waking thoughts, and I start from my sleep haunted with the question, Eternity, and where shall I spend it." "I cannot help you," Dr. Winslow quietly replied. "What," exclaimed the young man, "you cannot help me? Have I come all the way from Paris to London, to have my last hope taken away." "No," replied Dr. Winslow, "I cannot help you, but I can tell you of a Physician that can." He walked across his office and took from the table a Bible and pointed to Isaiah 53:5 and read, " 'But He was wounded for our transgressions. He was bruised for our iniquities: the chastisement of our peace was upon Him; and with His stripes we are healed.' That is the only Physician in the universe who can help you, Jesus Christ." The lip of the young French nobleman curled with scorn. "What," he said, "do you mean to tell me, Dr. Forbes Winslow, that you, one of the leading scientists of the day, the most eminent pathologist in the diseases of the mind in the world, that you believe that effete superstition of Christianity?" "Yes," replied Dr. Winslow calmly, "I believe in Christ, and believing in Him has saved me from becoming what you are." The young Frenchman stood a moment in deep thought, then he looked up at Dr. Winslow and said, "Well if I am honest I ought at least to be ready to consider it, ought I not?" "Yes." "Well, will you be my teacher?" "Yes," replied Dr. Forbes Winslow, and the eminent pathologist in diseases of the mind became the physician of the soul. For several days he opened the Word of God about Christ and His salvation to the young nobleman until the light dawned in upon his soul, and his heart was at rest, and he went back to Paris with the great question settled of, Eternity, and where shall I spend it? Eternity, and where shall I spend it? ETERNITY, AND WHERE SHALL I SPEND IT? I thank God I know where I shall spend eternity. I shall spend it with Christ in glory.

Study Questions

1. Why is it important to ask the question: "Where shall I spend eternity?"?
2. What are the seven points R. A. Torrey makes in this chapter?

9

Which Shall We Believe, God or Man?

For what if some did not believe? Shall their unbelief make the faith of God without effect? God forbid: yea, let God be true, but every man a liar (Rom. 3:3, 4).

W hat I say tonight is going to save some of you, and it is going to damn some of you. Some of you are going to heed the truth and repent. Some of you are going to harden your hearts against the truth, and this will come up against you in the day of judgment. Our subject is, Which Shall We Believe, God or Man? You will find the text in Romans 3:3, 4, "For what if some did not believe? Shall their unbelief make the faith of God without effect? God forbid: yea, let God be true, but every man a liar."

I. God's Word Better Than Man's Word

My main proposition tonight is that God's word is better than man's. We live in a day when men are disposed to put great faith in what men say, especially in what learned men say, but little or no faith in what God says. Let some great man of science announce some discovery and no matter how incredible it may appear, no matter how much there is about it that we cannot understand, we believe it at once. But let a man find something in the Word of God that is contrary to his notions, or that has something in it that he cannot understand, and he discards it at once. Tell men what the Bible says, and they look wise and shrug their shoulders and say, "Yes, but I do not think so. I think this way." Tell them what some great scientist or some leading literary critic, or some brilliant but erratic preacher says, and they think that settles it. What foolishness, what consummate foolishness. The opinion of the greatest scientist that ever lived, or the greatest philosopher, or the most learned Hebrew or Greek scholar, or the most brilliant pulpit orator is of no value whatever against the word of the infinitely wise and eternally truthful God, of God who is never mistaken and cannot lie. The opinion of all men together is of no weight against the Word of God. "Let God be true, and every man a liar." The man who believes any man against God is a fool. The man who believes any company of men against God is a fool. The Bible is the Word of God. That can be proven by many unanswerable proofs. I have proven it from this platform. On the other hand, for eighteen centuries and more the opinions of scientists and philosophers have come and gone, today regarded as the final word of wisdom, and tomorrow regarded as sheerest folly. But the teachings of this Book for all these centuries have stood fast amid all the wreckage of man's thinking. The experience of eighteen centuries proves that the man who banks on the Bible is wise. The man who throws the Bible overboard and turns to any other source of light and guidance always misses it in the long run. He always has for eighteen centuries, and he always will for all the centuries that are to come. The truly wise man is he who always believes this Book against the opinion of any man, against any scientist, against any philosopher, against any literary scholar, against any council of theologians or any congress of philosophers and savants. If the Bible says one thing and any body of men, or any company of men say another, the truly wise man will say, "Let God be true, but every man a liar."

II. Some Points on Which Men Differ from God

1. *Let us look at some points at which many men differ from God. First of all, a great many men, men who are considered wise, unusually wise, differ from God about the existence of a personal devil.* A very large number of men in our day, including some prominent theologians, laugh at the idea of their being any such person as the devil. One frequently hears men say, "There is no devil but sin." Now that is what men say, very many men, but what does God say? Turn to Ephesians 6:11, 12 and you will see what God says: "Put on the whole armor of God, that

ye may be able to stand against the wiles of *the devil*. For our wrestling is not against flesh and blood, but against the principalities, against the powers, against the world-rulers of this darkness, against the spiritual hosts of wickedness in the heavenly places." Turn to 1 Peter 5:8 and you will see again what God has to say on this point. He says, "Be sober, be watchful: *your adversary the devil* as a roaring lion, walketh about, seeking whom he may devour." God says that there is a devil, a being of great cunning and great power, as well as great malignity, a being who is more than a match for you or me, and that he is plotting our destruction and all the time working to accomplish it. God is certainly right about this, and, if you believe there is no devil but your own sin you are a greatly deceived individual, and the very devil you think does not exist has deceived you, and he has done it in order to destroy you. An Indian in ambush is a particularly dangerous Indian and a devil who has persuaded people that he does not exist at all is a particularly dangerous devil. No other class of people fall so easily a prey to the devil's subtlety as do the people who do not believe there is any devil. Show me a man or woman who does not believe there is a devil, and I will show you every time a man or woman whom the devil has blinded and on whom he is getting in his work. The Christian Scientists are among the leaders of those who deny the existence of a personal devil, and what other class of intelligent people are there on earth today who are so evidently blinded by the devil as they are. Many of the Christian Scientists are people of unusual intelligence in many matters, but when they come to talk about their peculiar theories their reasoning is the most absurd that was ever foisted upon a credulous and devil-blinded people.

2. *Many men differ from God about a future judgment.* Many and many in this day do not believe that there is to be a future judgment. Tell many men in our day that there is a time coming when they shall have to stand before the judgment bar of God with His holy and all-seeing eye piercing them through and through, and answer for all their deeds done in the body, and for all their words that they have spoken; tell them that for every idle word a man speaks he will have to give account thereof in the day of judgment, as the Lord Jesus Christ says they will (Matt. 12:36), and they will laugh at you in scorn. But what does God say? Turn to Acts 17:30, 31 and you will find what God says. "The times of ignorance therefore God overlooked; but now He

commandeth men that they should all everywhere repent: inasmuch as He hath appointed a day in which He will judge the world in righteousness by the man whom He hath ordained; whereof He hath given assurance unto all men, in that He hath raised Him from the dead." Turn to Romans 14:12 and you will hear what God has to say on this subject, "So then each one of us shall give account of himself to God." Turn to 2 Corinthians 5:10 and you will hear again what God has to say, "For we must all appear before the judgment seat of Christ, that every one may receive the things done in his body, according to that he hath done, whether it be good or bad." Turn once more to Matthew 12:36 and you will hear God's very plain utterance on this subject spoken by the lips of His own Son, our Lord and Savior Jesus Christ, "And I say unto you, that every idle word that men shall speak, they shall give account thereof in the day of judgment." God is right again. There is one thing absolutely sure about the future and that is that there is going to be a judgment day. How this present war will turn out I do not know and no other man knows. A few weeks ago we were told that it was absolutely sure that Germany would be conquered in three months, but now they are telling us that it will take three years, and the fact is we do not know that it will be conquered at all. It is not absolutely sure. It is not absolutely sure that there will ever be another summer or another election or another Christmas, but it is sure that there will be a judgment day. It is asolutely sure that you and I will stand before the judgment seat of Christ and give account of the deeds done here in the body, and the words spoken here. It is absolutely sure that each one of us will give account of himself to God.

3. *Many men differ from God about hell.* (1) There are many in our day who do not believe that there is any hell at all. There are many who say in the most positive way, "There is no hell." A lady once said to me, "Why, Mr. Torrey, you do not believe in hell?" It is not a question what I believe, but what God says. What does God say? He says in Matthew 5:29, 30, which by the way is a part of the Sermon on the Mount which all men say they believe, even though they do not believe the rest of the Bible: "And if thy right eye causeth thee to stumble, pluck it out, and cast it from thee: for it is profitable for thee that one of thy members should perish, and not thy whole body be cast into hell. And if thy right hand causeth thee to stumble, cut it off, and cast it from thee: for it is profitable for thee that one of thy members

should perish, and not thy whole body go into hell." I have quoted these words of God from the Revised Version, for many foolishly say that hell while it is found in the King James Version has disappeared from the Revised Version. They evidently know as little about the Revised Version as they do about the King James. Again you will find what God says on this subject in Luke 12:4, 5, "And I say unto you my friends, Be not afraid of them that kill the body, and after that have no more that they can do. But I will warn you whom ye shall fear: Fear him, who after he hath killed hath power to cast into hell; yea, I say unto you, Fear him." Let me say in passing that the one who has power to cast into hell is not the devil. The devil has no power to cast into hell nor in hell—in hell he himself is one of the prisoners. God is the One who has power to cast into hell and He is the One whom we should fear. Turn once more to Revelation 21:8, and you will see a very plain statement of God about hell: "But the fearful, and unbelieving, and abominable, and murderers, and fornicators, and sorcerers and idolaters, and all liars, shall have their part in the lake that burneth with fire and brimstone; which is the second death."

(2) There are some again who believe there is a hell, but they do not believe it is an everlasting hell. Many say, "You do not believe in everlasting punishment, do you?" Again I say it is not a question of what I believe, or what you believe, but of what God says. Read Matthew 25:41, "Then shall he say unto them on the left hand, Depart from me, ye cursed, into the eternal fire which is prepared for the devil and his angels." As to how long that punishment lasts that is prepared for the devil and his angels, you will find it set forth in Revelation 20:10, which describes what will occur at the end of the millennium, after the beast and the false prophet have been in hell a thousand years: "And the devil that deceived them was cast into the lake of fire and brimstone, where are also the beast and the false prophet [remember they have already been there 1,000 yrs.]; and they shall be tormented day and night *forever and ever*." Listen again to what God says in Revelation 14:9–1,

And the third angel followed them, saying with a loud voice, If any man worship the beast and his image, and receive his mark in his forehead, or in his hand, the same shall drink of the wine of the wrath of God, which is poured out without mixture into the cup of his indignation; and he shall be tormented with fire and brimstone in the presence of the holy angels, and in the presence of the Lamb, and the smoke of their torment ascendeth up *forever and ever:* and they have no rest day nor night, who worship the beast and his image, and whosoever receiveth the mark of his name.

Listen once more to what God has to say on the subject of eternal hell in Revelation 20:15, "And if any was not found written in the book of life, he was cast into the lake of fire." Is your name written in the Book of Life? If it is not, you will spend an endless eternity in hell. I do not state that as my opinion, but as God's Word. Make it sure tonight that your name is in the Book of Life by accepting Jesus Christ.

4. *Again men differ from God about a future probation.* There are many men who say, and they are oftentimes men whom the world considers wise, and they say it with great positiveness, that if men do not repent of their sins and accept Christ now in this life, they will have another chance to repent and turn to Christ after they are dead. I formerly believed and preached that myself, but what does God say? Turn to John 8:21 and you will find what God says. God tells us that the Lord Jesus Christ said unto the people that gathered around Him when He was here on earth, "I go away, and ye shall seek me, and shall die in your sin: where I go, ye cannot come." In other words, God says through His Son, the Lord Jesus Christ, that if a man dies in his sin he cannot go where Jesus Christ does, that he has no other chance. Turn again to Hebrews 9:27 and read what God says about a future probation: "It is appointed unto men once to die, but after this cometh judgment." Listen once more to what God has to say about a future probation. You will find it in 2 Corinthians 5:10, "For we must all appear before the judgment seat of Christ that every one may receive the things done in his body, according to that he hath done, whether it be good or bad." Note that carefully. The basis of judgment will be *"the things done in the body,"* the things done in this present life, the things done before we shuffle off this mortal coil, the things done this side of the grave. When a man's life on earth is ended, his eternal destiny is settled.

5. *Men differ from God about the way of salvation.* Many men say that if a man lives a good moral life he will be saved; he may be a Jew or a Mohammedan, or a Buddhist, or a Christian, but if he is only sin-

cere he will be saved. They say no man will be lost simply because he does not believe in Jesus Christ and confess Jesus Christ before the world. At the time of Col. Ingersoll's death a Chicago preacher who claimed to be a Christian said, "Heaven or any good country will welcome a man like Col. Ingersoll." Of course, the infidels applauded when he said it, and I suppose that this professedly Christian preacher was glad to get the applause of the avowed enemies of Jesus Christ. But what does God say? Listen to John 14:6, "Jesus saith unto him, I am the Way, the Truth and the Life: no man cometh unto the Father but by me." Listen again to what God says in Acts 4:12, "Neither is there salvation in any other [than Jesus Christ]: for there is none other name under heaven given among men whereby we must be saved." Listen still again as God speaks in John 3:18, "He that believeth on Him [i.e., on Jesus Christ] is not condemned: but he that believeth not is condemned already, *because he hath not believed on the name of the only begotten Son of God.*" Listen still again to the voice of God as He speaks to us in John 3:36, "He that believeth on the Son hath everlasting life: and he that believeth not the Son shall not see life: but the wrath of God abideth on him." Listen still again as God speaks in Romans 10:9, 10, "If thou shalt confess with thy mouth Jesus as Lord, and shalt believe in thy heart that God raised Him from the dead, thou shalt be saved: for with the heart man believeth unto righteousness; and with the mouth confession is made unto salvation." Listen once again, and now God is speaking through the lips of His Son, Jesus Christ, (Matt. 10:32, 33), "Every one therefore who shall confess me before men, him will I also confess before my Father who is in heaven. But whosoever shall deny me before men, him will I also deny before my Father who is in heaven."

6. *Many men differ from God about the conditions of entering the kingdom of God.* Many men say that the way to get into the kingdom of God is by leading an upright life, by treating your wife well, and your children well, and being honest in business, and kind to the poor, and doing other good things. Others say the way to enter the kingdom of God is by being baptized and uniting with the church and partaking of the communion, and reading your Bible, and saying your prayers, and going to confession, and so forth. But what does God say? Listen, John 3:3, 5, "Jesus answered, and said unto him, Verily, verily I say unto thee, *Except a man be born of water and of the Spirit,* he cannot

enter into the kingdom of God." Listen again on the same point to the voice of God as He speaks in Titus 3:5, 6, "Not by works done in righteousness, which we did ourselves, but according to His mercy He saved us, through the washing of regeneration and renewing of the Holy Spirit, which He poured out upon us richly, through Jesus Christ our Savior."

7. *Men differ from God about the best time to repent and accept Christ.* Many men are saying that there will be some day a better time than tonight to repent of our sins and to turn to Christ. Many of you here tonight are saying that, or thinking it if you do not say it, or acting it if you do not think it. But what does God say? Listen. Second Corinthians 6:2, "Behold, *now* is the accepted time, behold *now is the day of salvation.*" Listen again, Hebrews 3:7, "The Holy Ghost saith *today.*" Listen still again (Prov. 27:1), "Boast not thyself of tomorrow; for thou knowest not what a day may bring forth." And now listen once more (Prov. 29:1), "He that being often reproved hardeneth his neck shall suddenly be destroyed, and that without remedy." When the apostle Paul reasoning before Felix, the corrupt Roman governor, told him of righteousness and self-control, and the judgment to come, Felix was terrified, but he thought there would be a better time to repent than just then, and said, "Go thy way for this time, when I have a convenient season, I will call for thee." He thought some other time would be more convenient than that time, but he never found the more convenient time, and that is why he is in hades now and why he will spend eternity in hell.

These are some of the things that men say and some of the things God says. Which will you believe I say, "Let God be true, and every man a liar." But perhaps someone will say, "But I do not believe that the Bible is the Word of God." My friend, did it ever occur to you that your not believing that the Bible is the word of God does not alter the fact at all? At the time of the Boxer uprising in China some of the Boxers did not believe they could be killed by bullets; they thought that their incantations and their magic rites made them invulnerable against bullets. They were very sincere in their belief. A Chinese officer asked them to prove their sincerity by drawing up in line, and he would have his soldiers shoot at them. They consented. They drew up in line before the muzzles of the guns. They were very sincere. The Chinese soldiers blazed away, and every Boxer dropped dead. Their doubt of the power of the bullets to kill them did not alter the fact. Your doubt that the Bible is God's Word does not alter the fact that it is. Suppose for a moment that the Bible turns out to be the Word of God, as all those who know it best and know God best say that it is. You must at least admit that it is possible that it is the Word of God. You must admit that the men and women who are really living nearest God and know God best believe that the Bible is the Word of God. Suppose they prove to be right, where will you be? Damned. And that is exactly what you will be if you go on doubting God's Word and rejecting God's Son, listening to the voice of man rather than the voice of God.

God says that there is a devil and that you need Christ's help against his cunning and power. God says that there is a future judgment and that we must all give account to God. God says that there is a hell, and that it is a place of torment where all who reject Christ will spend eternity. God says there is no future probation, that the issues of eternity are settled in the life that now is. God says there is but one way to be saved, that is, by the acceptance of Jesus Christ as our Savior, and surrender to Him as our Lord, and confession of Him before the world. God says that the only way to enter the kingdom is to be born-again. God says that the best time to accept Christ and be saved is right now. "Now is the accepted time; now is the day of salvation." "The Holy Ghost saith today." "Boast not thyself of tomorrow, for thou knowest not what a day may bring forth." "He that being often reproved hardeneth his neck shall suddenly be destroyed, and that without remedy." Who of you will turn from sin and unbelief and turn to Jesus Christ and accept Him as your Savior and surrender to Him as your Lord and Master, and confess Him as such right now?

Study Questions

1. Why is God's Word better than man's word?
2. List at least five ways in which men differ from God.

10

The New Birth As Set Forth in John 3:2–21

The subject of our study this morning is The New Birth. One of the most fundamental and vital doctrines in Christianity is the doctrine of the new birth. If men are wrong here, they are likely to be wrong everywhere, and if they are right and clear in regard to this doctrine, they are pretty sure to be right and clear on every doctrine. We shall study the doctrine of the new birth as it is set forth in the third chapter of John, the 1st to 21st verses. In this chapter our Lord tells us first of the Necessity of the New Birth; second, the Nature of the New Birth, and third, the Method of the New Birth.

I. The Necessity of the New Birth

1. The first thing that our Lord Jesus teaches us in the third chapter of John in regard to the necessity of the new birth is that the necessity is UNIVERSAL. In the third verse He says, "Verily, verily I say unto thee, except a man be born again, he cannot see the kingdom of God." Literally translated, these words would read, "Verily, verily, I say unto thee, except anyone be born again [or, from above], he cannot see the kingdom of God." Not one single man or woman or child will be able to see the kingdom of God except they be born from above. In verse 7 our Lord says, "Marvel not that I said unto *thee, Ye* must be born again [or from above]." The emphasis is upon the "thee" and "Ye." Nicodemus would not have been at all amazed or surprised if the Lord Jesus had taught that a Gentile needed to be born-again; what surprised him was that the Lord should have said it to

him, and that he and other men of his class must be born-again. Our Lord's words when taken in their connection, set forth in the most forcible manner possible that there is not one single man on earth who can see the kingdom of God except he have a personal experience of the new birth. If any man could get to heaven without being born-again, Nicodemus was the man. He seemed to have pretty much everything that would entitle one to an entrance into the kingdom of God. He was a man of most scrupulous morality, he was a man of lofty aspirations, he was a man who longed to know the truth and was willing to make sacrifices in order to know it, he was a man who was endeavoring to live up to the truth as far as he did know it, he was a generous man, giving a tithe of all that he got as a starting point in his giving, and added to that generous freewill offerings; he was an intensely religious man, a man who studied his Bible, and a man who prayed, he was a man who carefully observed the ceremonials of the Jewish religion (which was a divinely revealed religion, John 4:22), he was an active worker, he was a teacher of the truth as far as he knew it, indeed he was *"the* teacher of Israel." What more could a man need in order to fit him to see and enter the kingdom of God? And yet the Lord Jesus said to him, *"You* need to be born again." If Nicodemus could not see nor enter the kingdom without the experience of the new birth, certainly none of us can. The necessity of the new birth is absolutely universal; there are no exceptions. The teaching is very common today that while certain classes of men and women, those that have gone into sin and whose characters have become corrupted, may need to be born-again, people who are well born the first time, of pious parents, and who have a naturally amiable disposition, and who have been reared morally and religiously from early childhood, do not need to be born-again. The Lord Jesus Christ says that they do. Not one man, woman or child shall see or enter the kingdom of God without being born-again.

2. The seventh verse teaches us that the necessity of the new birth is not only universal, but that it is also IMPERATIVE. Our Lord Jesus says to Nicodemus, "You *must* be born again," not merely you *may* be, but "you *must* be." The new birth is not merely a matter of privilege, it is a matter of solemn and imperative necessity, and I say to every one of you here today, who has not already been born-again, "You *must* be born again."

3. The third thing that Jesus taught regarding the necessity of the new birth is that it is also ABSOLUTE. Nothing else will take the place of the new birth. (1) *Reform* will not take the place of the new birth. Many of the preachers of our day are preaching reform; they are telling men, and tell men very forcefully, that they must give up this sin and that sin in their lives. Well, reform is well enough in its way, but mere reform will not save, no matter how thoroughgoing the reform may be. Men need something deeper and more radical than reform, they must be *"born again."* The central teaching of one great preacher in this land was "Quit your meanness," and he led thousands of people in this country to quit their meanness in many forms, but quitting one's meanness is not enough, however desirable it may be, as far as it goes. What men need to be told is, "You must be *born again."* There must be not mere reformation but regeneration.

(2) *Morality* is not enough. Morality is an attractive thing, but it is an external thing. Nicodemus had morality, but he needed something more, something deeper, something that underlies a true and abiding morality. Our Lord said (Matt. 5:20), "I say unto you, that except your righteousness shall exceed the righteousness of the scribes and Pharisees, ye shall in no wise enter into the kingdom of heaven." The Pharisees were moral, scrupulously moral, but their morality was superficial; it was not a morality of the heart. The only man who will enter into the kingdom of heaven is the man whose morality is of that deep kind, affecting the will and the affections and the whole inner life, that results from the new birth.

(3) *Baptism* will not take the place of the new birth. In the fifth verse we are told, "Except a man be born of water *and the Spirit*, he cannot enter into the kingdom of God." Even if we take the water in this passage to refer to the water of baptism (which it does not) still we find our Lord saying that it is not enough to be born of water, but that we must be born, "of water *and the Spirit."* The birth from above, the birth by the power of the Holy Ghost, is necessary, even though one has been baptized by water in any form of baptism. In the 8th chapter of Acts we read of Simon Magus who was baptized, and whatever the proper form of baptism may be, he was certainly baptized by the proper form for the work was done by a divinely appointed man, and yet further on in the record we hear Peter saying unto this same properly baptized Simon Magus, "Thou hast neither

part nor lot in this matter: for *thy heart is not right before God. . . .* For I see that *thou art in the gall of bitterness and in the bond of iniquity.*" The baptism of Simon Magus was not enough, it was not the new birth, and he needed to be born-again. (4) *Religion* will not take the place of the new birth. Religion is all right in its way, if it is true religion, but religion will not save. No amount of observation of the externalities of true religion, Bible reading, prayer, churchgoing, observation of the ordinances, will save. No man can see or enter the kingdom of heaven, no matter how religious, except he be born-again. Nicodemus was religious, extremely religious, but he was unsaved until he was born-again. (5) *Generosity* in giving will not take the place of the new birth. How many there are today who are really depending for their hope of heaven upon their generous giving, and how many there are who think of others who are generous givers that these men cannot be lost because they give so much for the poor and for God's work, but even though one should give all his goods to feed the poor, and have not that love which comes from being born-again it would profit him nothing (1 Cor. 13:3). The Pharisees were generous givers, they were careful to tithe absolutely everything they received, down to the mint and anise in their gardens, but they were unsaved and needed to be born-again. (6) *Conviction of sin* will not take the place of the new birth. Many think that they are saved because by the power of the Holy Spirit they have been brought under deep conviction of sin, but after they have spent days or weeks in agony over their sins they find that conviction is not conversion, much less is it the new birth, and though one should sob and wail over his sins for years or his whole life, he could not by that means enter the kingdom of heaven. No amount of sobbing and wailing and doing penance will take the place of the new birth. (7) *Culture* will not take the place of the new birth, even though it be "ethical culture" or religious culture. Everywhere through Christendom the churches are substituting culture, "ethical culture," or religious culture, or intellectual culture, for the new birth, but culture will not do: "you *must be born again.*" Nicodemus was one of the most cultured men among his people; he was *"the teacher* of Israel," but he was lost, and the most cultured people of America today, the most cultured men and women of Los Angeles are lost men and women, unless they have been born-again. (8) *Prayer* will not take the place of the new birth. A man may spend hours a day in prayer and yet be a lost man. Cornelius was a man of prayer and a generous giver, so notable was he for prayer and alms-giving that his prayers and alms went up for a remembrance before God (Acts 10:4), but he needed to be saved by being born-again through faith in Jesus Christ, and the angel said to him to send to Joppa for a man called Peter who would speak unto him words whereby he should "be *saved*" (Acts 11:13, 14). Evidently he was not saved as yet. The necessity of the new birth is absolute; there is nothing else that will take its place.

4. *Why is the new birth absolutely necessary?* Verse 6 tells us why the new birth is absolutely necessary, why nothing else will take its place. The reason is because "that which is born of the flesh is flesh; and that which is born of the Spirit is spirit." In other words, all that we can get by our human parentage, no matter how godly or pious or moral or cultured our parentage may be, is that which is natural and not that which is spiritual, and the kingdom of God is spiritual and in order to enter that kingdom we must be born of the Spirit. Human nature is rotten to the core.

II. The Nature of the New Birth

In this chapter we have a very clear explanation of just what the nature of the new birth is.

1. First of all it is a RADICAL TRANSFORMATION OF OUR INMOST NATURE. This comes out in the very wording of what our Lord said, "Ye must be *born* again [or, anew, or, from above]." It is not a mere outward change, but a *birth*, a new birth. Elsewhere we are told it is a new creation. Paul says in 2 Corinthians 5:17, "If any man is in Christ, he is a *new creation* [or, there is a new creation]: the old things are passed away; behold they are become new." Evidently the new birth is a radical transformation in the deepest depths of our being, the impartation of a new nature, a new intellectual nature, a new emotional nature, a new volitional nature. That is to say, new thoughts, new ideas, new ambitions, new desires, new feelings, new emotions, a new will. It is an impartation of God's own nature to us. As the apostle Peter puts it in 2 Peter 1:4, "By these [that is by the Word of God, by God's exceeding great and precious promises]" we "become partakers of the divine nature." We are born into this world with a corrupt nature in

every part of our mental and moral being. Our minds are blind to the truth of God. As Paul puts it, "the natural man receiveth not the things of the Spirit of God for they are foolishness unto him; and he cannot know them, because they are spiritually discerned" (1 Cor. 2:14); our feelings are corrupt, we love the things that God hates and hate the things that God loves; our will is perverse, our wills are set upon pleasing ourselves instead of upon pleasing God. In the new birth we get a new mind, a mind that is open to the truth of God, that thinks the thoughts of God after Him; we get new affections, we now love the things that God loves and hate the things that God hates; we get a new will, a will that is in harmony with the will of God, a will that is set upon pleasing God and not set upon pleasing self.

2. The new birth is also a BIRTH FROM ABOVE. We learn this from verses 3 and 7. Jesus said, "Verily, verily, I say unto thee, Except a man be born *from above*, he cannot see the kingdom of God." And again, "Marvel not that I said unto thee, Ye must be born from *above*." In our King James Version we find the words "born *again*," and in the Revised Version, "born *anew*," but a more exact translation is "born *from above*." The new birth is a birth from above, it is a heavenly birth, it is a birth from God, a direct work of God in the individual heart.

III. The Method of the New Birth, or How Men Are Born-again

We come now to the directly practical questions, how are men born-again, and what must we do in order to be born-again. This question is answered plainly in the chapter we are studying.

1. First of all *we are born-again by the Holy Spirit's power.* We read in verses 5 to 8, "Jesus answered, Verily, verily, I say unto thee, Except a man be born of water *and the Spirit*, he cannot enter into the kingdom of God." The new birth is the Holy Spirit's work. The Holy Spirit is a living person today who operates directly upon the spirits of men, quickening them, and by His transforming power working directly in our spirits we are regenerated. The Holy Spirit imparts a new nature to us.

2. The new birth, while wrought by the power of the Holy Spirit, *is wrought through the instrumentality of the Word of God.* This comes

out in the fifth verse, "Except a man be born *of water* and the Spirit, he cannot enter into the kingdom of God." There is reason to believe that the water here means the water of the Word, but we will not go into that at this time. Whether that is taught here or not, it certainly is taught elsewhere in the Bible. For example, we read in 1 Peter 1:23, "Being born-again, not of corruptible seed, but of incorruptible, *through the Word of God,* which liveth and bideth." And we read in James 1:18, "By His own will He brought us forth *by the word of truth,* that we should be a kind of first fruits of his creatures." The Spirit of God is the one who works the new birth; the Word of God is the instrument through which He does it. We preach the Word of God to men, God quickens it by the power of His Holy Spirit as we preach it, it takes root in the human heart, and the result is the new nature. If we wish to see others born-again, we should give them the Word of God in the power of the Holy Ghost, and the result will be that they will be born-again. If we have not been born-again ourselves we should read and ponder the Word of God, and while we do so look to the Holy Spirit to quicken it in our hearts, and the new birth will be the result.

3. The new birth is wrought by the Holy Spirit through His Word in *us when we look to or believe on Jesus Christ.* This comes out in verses 14 and 15. Nicodemus had asked the Lord how these things could be, and how one could be born when he is old, that is, how one could be born-again. Verses 14 and 15 contain the Lord's answer to the question He said, "And as Moses lifted up the serpent in the wilderness, even so must the Son of man be lifted up; that *whosoever believeth in Him* should not perish, but have eternal life." The Lord was referring to an incident in the Wilderness when the murmuring Israelites were bitten by fiery serpents and were dying from the bite, and Moses cried to God for deliverance and God commanded Moses to make a serpent of brass (in appearance like to the fiery serpent that had bitten them) and to put it on a pole and that it would come to pass that every one that was bitten when he looked at the serpent on the pole would live (Num. 21:5–9). We all have been bitten by the serpent of sin. His bite is death, eternal death. But the Lord Jesus Christ has been made in the likeness of sinful flesh and *"lifted up"* on the cross of Calvary where He made a perfect atonement for sin, and as soon as we look at Him on the cross and put our trust in Him as our

sin-bearer, that moment we are born-again. The same thought is found in the 16th verse, "For God so loved the world, that He gave His only begotten Son, that *whosoever believeth on Him* should not perish but have eternal life." All anyone has to do to be born-again is, to *look and live*, to look at Jesus Christ, putting his confidence in Him, to look at Christ crucified and put faith in Him as our atoning Savior, and the moment we do thus put our faith in Him, that moment the Spirit of God, through His Word, which presents Him to us as our atoning Savior, imparts to us God's own nature and we are born-again. The same thought is presented very clearly and very simply in the first chapter and the 12th and 13th verses, "As many as received Him (i.e., the Lord Jesus), to them gave He the right to become children of God, even to them that believe on His name: which were born, not of blood, nor of the will of the flesh, nor of the will of man, but of God." All anyone has to do then to be born-again is to receive Jesus Christ, to receive Him as that which He offers Himself to be to us: as our atoning Savior, who bore all our sins in His own body on the cross; as our risen Savior and Deliverer from the power of sin; as our Teacher sent from God, who spoke the very words of God; as our Lord and Master, who has a right to, and to whom we surrender, the absolute control of our lives; and as our divine Lord. If there is anyone here this morning who has never been born-again, all you have to do to be born-again is to thus receive Jesus this moment, and the moment you do so receive Him you will be born from above, born of God.

Study Questions

1. What does it mean that the new birth is universal?
2. What does it mean that the new birth is imperative?
3. What does it mean that the new birth is absolute?
4. Why doesn't baptism take the place of the new birth?
5. Describe the nature of the new birth.
6. How are men born-again?

11

God's Guidance and How to Get It

I will instruct thee and teach thee in the way which thou shalt go; I will guide thee with mine eye (Ps. 32:8).

But if any of you lacketh wisdom, let him ask God, who giveth to all men liberally, and upbraideth not; and it shall be given him. But let him ask in faith, nothing doubting; for he that doubteth is like the surge of the sea driven by the wind and tossed. For let not that man think that he shall receive anything of the Lord; a double-minded man, unstable in all his ways (James 1:5–8).

I. The Possibility and Blessedness of Being Guided by God

One of the greatest and most precious privileges of the believer is to have the guidance of God at every turn of life. One of the most important of all practical questions is how to get this guidance. There are many who say very positively that they are guided of God who are not so guided. The event proves that they are not so guided. Some months ago a young woman informed me that she was guided of God to leave for Africa at a certain date and that God had given her positive assurance that the money would be provided for her to leave at that date. I was not at all sure that she was guided as she said that she was, and the event proved she was not; for the money was not furnished for her to leave at that date. As we see so many people apparently absolutely sure that God is guiding them when in the event it becomes clear that He is not, does it not prove that the supposed guidance of God is a fancy and not a fact? It does not. The fact that some people are confident that they are guided when they are not is no more evidence that there is no such thing as guidance than the fact that some people are sure they are saved when they are not is an evidence that there is no such thing as salvation, or assurance of salvation. The fact that some people are misled in no way proves that all people are misled. There is such a thing as guidance, and there is a way to get guidance. There is a way to avoid the illusions regarding guidance into which many fall through ignorance of the Word of God.

II. How to Get Guidance

We come now face to face with the question of how to get God's guidance. There are seven steps, clearly set forth in the Word of God, in the path that leads to God's guidance.

1. The first step toward obtaining God's guidance is that we *accept the Lord Jesus Christ as our own personal Savior, and surrender to Him as our Lord and Master*. This comes out very plainly in James 1:5, "If any of *you* lacketh wisdom, let *him* ask of God." It is clear that the promise is only made to believers. James does not say, "If *any man* lacketh wisdom, let him ask of God," but, "If any of *you* lacketh wisdom, let him ask of God." There is no promise in the Word of God that God will guide anyone but the believer in Jesus Christ. Indeed there is no promise in the Word of God that He will answer the prayers of unbelievers about anything. God's guidance is the privilege of the believer in Jesus Christ and of him alone. By believer I do not mean the one who merely has an orthodox faith about Jesus Christ, but the one who is a believer in the Bible sense, that is, the one who has that living faith in Jesus Christ that leads him to receive Jesus Christ as his Lord and Savior, and to surrender his life to His service and control. If then, we would have God's sure guidance, the first thing to make sure of is that we really are believers, that we really are children of God, that we really have accepted Jesus Christ as our Savior, and really have surrendered our lives to His Lordship.

2. The second step toward obtaining God's guidance is that we *clearly realize our own utter inability to decide for ourselves the way in which we should go*. The promise, as we find it in the Word of God, makes this very plain. James says, "If any of you *lacketh wisdom*, let him ask of God, and so forth." *The promise is made to the one who lacks wisdom,*

not the one who has it. It is made to the one who realizes the limitations of his own wisdom and realizes his dependence upon God for His wisdom. It is at this point that many, very many, fail of guidance. They have such confidence in their own opinions, in their own judgment, in their own ability to decide the course that they should pursue, that though they may as a formality ask God for His guidance, they *do not really have any deep sense of their need of His guidance*, and they have such confidence in their own wisdom that they mistake their own judgment for the guidance of God. Having prayed for wisdom, but still being confident in their own judgment, they become all the more sure that their opinion is right, and they attribute their own opinion to God. If we are to have God's guidance, we must be utterly emptied of all confidence in our own judgment; and, in a sense of our own inability to decide for ourselves, we should come to God, putting our own notions utterly aside, for Him to tell us what He would have us to do, and we *should wait silently before Him to make known His will.*

3. The third step toward obtaining divine guidance is that we *really desire to know God's will, and are thoroughly willing to do it whatever it may be.* This also comes out in the promise. It reads, "If any of you lacketh wisdom, let him *ask of God.*" Of course, the *asking must be genuine*, and there is no genuine asking wisdom of God unless we are eagerly desirous of knowing God's will and heartily willing to do it when that will is made known. *The genuine and absolute surrender of the will to God is the great secret of guidance.* The promise, "I will instruct thee and teach thee in the way which thou shalt go; I will counsel thee with mine eye upon thee," as is evident from the context, is made to the one whose will is surrendered to God, for the next verse reads, "Be ye not as the horse, or as a mule, which have no understanding: whose trappings must be bit and bridle to hold them in, else they will not come unto thee." If we are *mulish*, that is, if we are bent on doing our own will, then God must guide us with "bit and bridle," and oftentimes must break our jaw before we submit to Him. His instruction, teaching and guidance, *His gentle guidance* "with His eye upon us," is for the one whose will is entirely surrendered to Him. The surrender must be *real* surrender. There are many who think they wish to know and are willing to do God's will, and that it is God's will that they are waiting to know, but, what they are really seeking, is to get God to say yes to their own plans, and get God to endorse the plan

they themselves have already subconsciously formed, and they are not waiting, as they suppose they are, until God tells them what His will really is, they are waiting until God tells them to do the thing that they want to do and, in their subconscious self, have made up their mind to do, so they think and think and think, and pray and pray and pray, until they think themselves into thinking that God tells them to do the thing that they themselves wished to do from the outset, and this thing that they wanted to do from the outset may not be God's plan at all. This is one of the most frequent causes of thinking we have the mind of God when we are only doing the thing that we want to do. Men and women who go to God for guidance in this way, that is, without having absolutely put aside their own will and their own opinion, when they do think themselves into the place where they fancy that God has endorsed their plan, are the most positive in saying that "God tells me to do thus and so." So then, we must, if we would be guided of God, make absolutely sure that we have put away our own will entirely and are utterly willing to and desirous of doing God's will, whatever it may be. *We must be sure that we are silent before God and truly listening to His voice,* and not still listening to this desire that we have in the depths of our heart that God shall tell us to do the thing that we want to do. When Mr. Moody invited me to take up the work in Chicago in 1889, I went to God to show me what might be His will. There was a great conflict in my heart. There were reasons why I wished to go to Chicago; there are reasons why I wished to stay in Minneapolis, or why I thought I must stay in Minneapolis. It took me three days to get absolutely silent before God, and to put away my own conflicting ideas on both sides. When I did come to the place where I had no will whatever in the matter, but simply wished to know what God's will was, whichever way it might be, when I became absolutely silent before God, God soon made the path in which He would have me go as plain as day.

The fact that the thing that we are contemplating doing is a hard thing, that it requires great sacrifice, does not by any means make it sure that it is God's will and not ours. Our hearts naturally are deceitful above all things, and oftentimes willful persons will set their heart on doing a very hard thing. They may set their heart upon doing it out of spiritual pride, or for many other reasons than because of surrender to the will of God. They want to do this hard thing, and they pray and pray, and brood and brood and brood until they make themselves think that this hard thing is the will of God, when very likely the thing that God would have them do is some very humdrum, everyday sort of a thing. There is many a man and many a woman determined to be a foreign missionary, and a foreign missionary under the most difficult circumstances, whom God has called to a very quiet life at home, and while they are willing to endure the severest hardships in the foreign field, they are not willing to plod on quietly and unseen and unnoticed at home. But the best thing is God's will, whether that will be in a quiet humdrum life at home, or whether it be a notable life of courage and self-sacrifice in the foreign field; and, if we are to have God's guidance, we must, as already said, become absolutely silent before God, and be willing and glad to serve Him in the most ordinary sort of life, a life that seems far beneath our talents and our training, if that be His will, just as ready to do that as to serve Him in a field that demands large abilities and great sacrifice. Satan cheats many of God's children out of accomplishing the things that God would have them do by making them restless in the homely paths that God opens up to them of doing things that they can do, and sets their heart upon doing things that they cannot do; and thus they leave the path of actual achievement to brood over things they would like to do, but which it is not God's will for them to do, and which they never will do. Oftentimes a whole life is spoiled in this way.

4. The fourth step toward obtaining God's guidance is *definite prayer for that guidance*. "If any of you lacketh wisdom," says God, "let him *ask of God*." There should be definite prayer for definite guidance. We should ask God's guidance at every turn of life; we should ask His guidance not merely in the great crises of life, but in the ordinary matters of everyday life; in our business, in our domestic work, in the most simple things. None of us knows enough to direct our own steps in the simplest matters of everyday life. We need God's guidance at every turn of life, and we can have it, and the way to get it is to ask for it. But the asking will do no good unless we have already taken the other steps that have been mentioned. The definite prayer is the fourth step and not the first, and we should be sure we have taken the first three steps before we take the fourth.

5. The fifth step toward obtaining God's guidance is *positive expectation that God will grant our prayer and give us the guidance that we*

ask. This also comes out in the exact wording of the promise. It reads, "If any of you lack wisdom, let him ask of God, who giveth to all men liberally, and upbraideth not, and it shall be given him. But *let him ask in faith, nothing doubting*: for he that doubteth is like the surge of the sea driven by the wind and tossed. For let not that man [i.e., the man that doubts, the man who does not confidently expect] think that he shall receive anything of the Lord." Here is where many miss God's guidance. Their wills are surrendered, they really desire to know and do God's will, and they ask God for His guidance, but they do not confidently expect that God will give the guidance they ask. They hope He will, but they are not at all sure that He will. If we have taken the other steps, when we ask God for His guidance we may be absolutely sure that God will give it. Someone may say, "But others have asked God's guidance and thought they had it, when the event showed they did not. May not I also be mistaken?" No, not if you have taken the other steps already mentioned and will take the steps that we are still to mention. We have God's absolute promise of guidance made to those who meet the conditions which we have described, and therefore we may ask guidance with the absolute certainty that we are going to receive it. When we ask for God's wisdom, if we are of those to whom the promise is made, we know that we have asked something according to God's will, for He has definitely promised it in His Word; and, therefore, we have a right to know that our prayer is heard and the thing we have asked is granted (1 John 5:14, 15). Some years ago I was speaking at a Bible Conference of the YMCA at White Bear Lake, Minnesota I was speaking on the subject of prayer. As I left the platform to hurry to a train I found the next speaker waiting for me on the outside of the audience. He was greatly excited. He was a gifted teacher of the Word of God and had been much used of God. He stopped me as I passed by hurrying to the train and said, "I am going to tear to pieces everything you have said to these young men." I replied, "If I have not spoken according to the Book I hope you will tear it to pieces, but what did I say that was not according to the Bible?" He answered, "You have produced upon these young men the impression that we can ask things of God and get the very thing we ask." I replied, "I do not know whether that is the impression I produced or not, but that is certainly the impression that I meant to produce." "But," he said, "that is not right. We should pray, 'if it be Thy will.' " "Yes," I replied, "if we do not know what the will of God is in the case we should say 'if it be Thy will,' but if God has revealed His will in any specific instance why should we put in any 'if?' " "But," he said, "we cannot know the will of God." "What is the Word of God given to us for," I asked, "if it is not to show us what the will of God is? For example, we are told in James 1:5–7, 'if any of you lacketh wisdom, let him ask of God, who giveth to all men liberally, and upbraideth not.' Now," I said, "when you ask for wisdom do you not know by this specific promise that you have asked something according to the will of God, and that you are going to get it?" "But," he replied, "I do not know what wisdom is." I said, "If you knew what wisdom was you would not need to ask for it, but whatever wisdom may be, do you not know that when you ask for wisdom God is going to give it?" He made no reply. What reply was there to make? Here we have a definite promise of God; and, if we meet the conditions of that promise, we may be, and ought to be, *absolutely sure*, that God will do as He says, absolutely sure that God will give us wisdom in this specific case in which we ask it. *If we have any uncertainty at this point, God will not give us the wisdom we ask.* We should rest absolutely on God's plain promise, and when we ask for wisdom be absolutely sure that wisdom is coming. How God gives wisdom we will consider later.

6. The sixth step toward obtaining God's guidance is to *follow God's guidance a step at a time as He gives it.* Here again is where many miss their way. Many seek to know the whole way before they take a single step, but God's method is to show us a step at a time. Look at Peter in Acts 12. God led him a step at a time: first the angel smote Peter on the side and awoke him, and told him to arise up quickly. This Peter did, and his chains fell from his hands. Then the angel said unto him, "Gird thyself and bind on thy sandals," and he did so. Then the angel said, "Cast thy garment about thee, and follow me," and Peter did exactly as he was told. He was not even sure that he was awake, but he followed step by step, even when he thought he might be asleep. They passed the first and second guard and came to the iron gate that led into the city. Peter did not stop and argue as to whether the gate would be opened or not, but just followed up to the gate, and when he got to the gate the gate opened of its own accord. Thus God led him step by step, and thus God leads us. The Word of God tells us that "The *steps* of a good man are ordered of the Lord" (Ps. 37:23).

The trouble with many of us is we wish God to show us the whole path, and are not willing to go a step at a time. Look at Paul in the 16th chapter of Acts, the 6th to 8th verses. Paul and his companions went through the region of Phrygia and Galatia and would have passed into the province of Asia to preach the Word there, but the Holy Ghost said, "No." So Paul passed over against Mysia and was about to go into Bithynia, the next province. At that point "the Spirit of Jesus" again said, "No"; so passing by Mysia he came down to Troas, and there a vision appeared to Paul in the night, leading him to go over into Macedonia. *Step by step* the Spirit led, and step by step Paul followed on. The thing for us to do is to *take the next step* that God shows us in answer to our prayer and not wait until God shows us the whole way. A college student once came to me at the Northfield Students' Convention, telling me that he was greatly perplexed as to his future life, that he had been asking God's guidance and could not get it. I asked Him what he was asking God's guidance about, and he said, about what he should do when he got out of college. I said, "How far are you along in college?" and he said that the following fall he would begin his junior year. I said, "Then you have two years left in college." "Yes." "Are you sure you ought to take those two years in college?" "Yes." "Then what you are perplexed about is because you cannot get guidance for two years from now." "Yes." "Well, just go on as God leads you, and in the two years if not before God will show you what to do next." A very large share of our perplexity about the will of God is of this kind. We are troubled because God has not shown us what He wants us to do next year, or it may be next month. All we need is God's guidance for today. *Follow on step by step as He leads you, and the way will open as you go.*

7. There remains just one more step in the path that leads to God's sure guidance, and that is that we *always bear in mind that God's guidance is clear guidance.* Here is where many go astray. They have impulses, they know not from what source; they have what appear like leadings for example, to go to the foreign field, or do some other thing, but they are not at all sure it is God's leading. Very likely it is not God's leading; and yet they follow it for fear they may be disobeying God, or, perhaps they do not follow it and then get into condemnation lest they have disobeyed God. I have met many in the deepest gloom from this cause. They had an impression they ought to do a cer-

tain thing, they were not at all clear the impression was from God, they did not do the thing, and then the devil has made them think that they have disobeyed God, and some even think they have committed the unpardonable sin because they did not obey this prompting (of the origin of which they were not at all sure). If we will only bear in mind that God's guidance is clear guidance, we will be delivered from this snare of Satan. We are told in John 1:5 that "God is light, and in Him is no darkness at all." Any leadings that are not absolutely clear, provided our wills are surrendered to God, are not from Him as yet. We have a right in every case where we have any impression that we ought to do a certain thing, but where we are not absolutely sure it is the will of God, to go to God and say to Him, "Heavenly Father, I desire to do Thy will; my will is absolutely surrendered to Thine, now if this is of Thee, make it clear as day, and I will do it," and if our wills are absolutely surrendered to God and we fully realize our own inability to decide and are ready to be led by Him, God will make as clear as day if it is His will, and we *have a right not to do it until He does make it clear, and we have a right to have an absolutely clear conscience in not doing it until He does make it clear.* God is a Father and is more willing to make His will known to us than we are to make our will known to our children, provided we really wish to know and wish to do His will. We have no right to be in mortal dread before God and to be in constant apprehension that we have not done His will. When we accepted Christ and surrendered our wills to God we did "not receive the spirit of bondage again unto fear," but the Spirit that gives us the place as sons where we cry, "Abba, Father," in perfect childlike trust in Him (Rom. 8:15). We would not mislead our children in such a case, we would not leave our children to any doubts or uncertainty, we would make our will as clear as day, and so will God make His. Satan will prevent a man or woman making a full surrender to God just as long as he can, but when a man does make a full surrender, then the devil will do everything in his power to torment him. He will suggest all kinds of ridiculous things for him to do, and then the man will not do them, and Satan will torment him by making him think he has gone back on his surrender to God. Let us never forget that *not all spiritual impressions are from the Holy Spirit.* There are other spirits besides the Holy Spirit, and we need to try the spirits whether they be of God (1 John 4:1). Some people are so anxious to be led of the Holy Spirit that they are willing to be led by any spirit and thus plunge into the delusions of spiritualism or "the tongues" business or other forms of fanaticism. I repeat it again, God's guidance is clear guidance, and *we should not follow any impression until God makes it as clear as day* that it is from Him.

The main point in the whole matter of guidance is the absolute surrender of the will to God, the delighting in His will and the being willing to do joyfully the very things we would not like to do naturally, the very things in connection with which there may be many disagreeable circumstances because of association with or even subordination to people that we do not altogether like, and difficulties of other kinds, doing them joyfully simply because it is the will of God, and the willingness to let God lead in any way He pleases, whether it may be by His Word or by His Spirit. If we will only completely distrust our own judgment and have absolute confidence in God's judgment, and God's willingness to guide us, and are absolutely surrendered to His will, whatever it may be, and are willing to let God choose His way of guidance, and will go on step by step as He does guide us, and are studying His word to know His will, and are listening for the still small voice of the Spirit, going step by step as He leads, He will guide us with His eye. He will guide us with His counsel to the end of our earthly pilgrimage, and afterwards receive us into glory (Ps. 73:24).

Study Questions

1. List the seven steps we should take in order to get God's guidance.

12

How God Guides

Nevertheless I am continually with thee: thou hast holden my right hand. Thou shalt guide me with thy counsel, and afterward receive me to glory (Ps. 73:23, 24).

Two weeks ago this morning we considered the question of God's guidance and how to obtain it. We have today a closely related subject, How God Guides. There are no promises of God's Word more precious to the man who wishes to do His will, and who realizes the goodness of His will, than the promises of His guidance. What a cheering, gladdening, inspiring thought that contained in the text is, that we may have the guidance of infinite wisdom and love at every turn of life and that we have it to the end of our earthly pilgrimage.

There are few more precious words in the whole book of Psalms, which is one of the most precious of all the books of the Bible, than these: "Thou hast holden my right hand. Thou shalt guide me with thy counsel, and afterwards receive me to glory." How the thoughtful and believing and obedient heart burns as it reads these wonderful words of the text. I wish we had time to dwell upon the characteristics of God's guidance as they are set forth in so many places in the Word of God, but we must turn at once to consideration of the means God uses in guiding us.

I. God Guides by His Word

First of all God guides by His word. We read in Psalm 119:105, "Thy *word* is a lamp unto my feet, and a light unto my path," and in the 130th verse of this same Psalm we read, "The entrance of *thy words* giveth light; it giveth understanding unto the simple." God's own written Word is the chief instrument that God uses in our guidance. God led the children of Israel by a pillar of cloud by day and a pillar of fire by night. The written Word, the Bible, is our pillar of cloud and fire. As it leads we follow. One of the main purposes of the Bible, the Word of God, is practical guidance in the affairs of everyday life. All other leadings must be tested by the Word. Whatever promptings may come to us from any other source, whether it be by human counsel, or by the prompting of some invisible spirit, or in whatever way it may come, we must test the promptings, or the guidance or the counsel by the sure Word of God, "To the law and to the testimony; if they speak not according to this Word, it is because there is no light in them" (Is. 8:20). Whatever spirit or impulse may move us, whatever dream or vision may come to us, or whatever apparently providential opening we may have, all must be tested by the Word of God. If the impulse or leading, or prompting, or vision, or providential opening is not according to the Book, it is not of God. "The prophet that hath a dream, let him tell a dream; and he that hath my Word, let him speak my Word faithfully. What is the *chaff* to the *wheat?* saith the LORD" (Jer. 23:28). If Christians would only study the Word, they would not be misled as they so often are by seducing spirits, or by impulses of any kind, that are not of God but of Satan or of their own deceitful hearts. How often people have said to me that the Spirit was leading them to do this or that, when the thing that they were being led to do was in direct contradiction to God's Word. For example, a man once called upon me to consult me about marrying a woman who he said was a beautiful Christian, and that they had deep sympathy in the work of God, and *the Spirit of God* was leading them to marry one another. "But," I said to the man, "you already have one wife." "Yes," he replied, "but you know we have not gotten on well together." "Yes," I said, "I know that, and furthermore, I have had a conversation with her and believe it is your fault more than hers. But, however that may be, if you should put her away and marry this other woman, Jesus Christ says that you would be an adulterer." "Oh, but," he replied, "the Spirit of God is leading us to one another." Now whatever spirit may have been leading that man, it certainly was not the Spirit of God, for the Spirit of God cannot lead anyone to do that which is in direct contradiction to the Word of God. I replied to this man: "You are a liar and a blasphemer. How dare you attribute to the Spirit of God action that is directly contrary to the teaching of Jesus Christ?" Many, many times Christian people have promptings from various sources which they attribute to the Holy Spirit, but which are in plain and flat contradiction to the clear and definite teachings of God's Word. The truth is, many so neglect the Word that they are all in a maze regarding the impulses and leadings that come to them, as to whence they are; whereas, if they studied the Word, they would at once detect the real character of these leadings.

But *the Word itself must be used in a right way if we are to find the leading of God from it.* We have no right to seek guidance from the Word of God by using it in any fantastic way, as some do. For example, there is no warrant whatever in the Word of God for trying to find out God's will by opening the Bible at random and putting our finger on some text without regard to its real meaning as made clear by the context. There is no warrant whatever in the Bible for any such use of it. The Bible is not a talisman, or a fortune-telling book, it is not in any sense a magic book; *it is a revelation from an infinitely wise God, made in a reasonable way, to reasonable beings*, and we obtain God's guidance from the Bible by taking the verse of Scripture in which the guidance is found, in the connection in which it is found in the Bible, and interpreting it, led by the Holy Spirit, in its context as found in the Bible. Many have fallen into all kinds of fanaticism by using their Bible in this irrational and fantastic way. Some years ago a prediction was made by a somewhat prominent woman Bible teacher that on a certain date Oakland and Alameda and some other California cities, and I think also Chicago, were to be swallowed up in an earthquake. The definite day was set and many were in anticipation, and many in great dread. A friend of mine living in Chicago was somewhat disturbed over the matter and sought God's guidance by opening her Bible at random, and this was the passage to which she opened: Ezekiel 12:17–28,

Moreover the word of the Lord came to me saying,

Son of man, eat thy bread with quaking, and drink thy water with trembling and with carefulness;

And say unto the people of the land, Thus saith the Lord GOD of the inhabitants of Jerusalem, and of the land of Israel: They shall eat their bread with carefulness, and drink their water with astonishment, that her land may be desolate from all that is therein, because of the violence of all them that dwell therein.

And the cities that are inhabited shall be laid waste, and the land shall be desolate; and ye shall know that I am the LORD.

And the word of the LORD came unto me, saying,

Son of man, what is that proverb that ye have in the land of Israel, saying, *The days are prolonged, and every vision faileth?*

Tell them therefore, Thus saith the LORD God; I will make this proverb to cease, and they shall no more use it as a proverb in Israel; but say unto them, *The days are at hand,* and *the effect of every vision.*

For there shall be no more any vain vision nor flattering divination within the house of Israel. For I am the LORD: I will speak, and the word that I shall speak shall come to pass; *it shall be no more prolonged:* for in your days, O rebellious house will I say the word, and will perform it, saith the Lord GOD.

Again the word of the LORD came to me, saying,

Son of man, behold they of the house of *Israel say, The vision that he seeth is for many days to come,* and *he prophesieth of the times that are far off.*

Therefore say unto them, Thus saith the Lord God; There *shall none of my words be prolonged anymore, but the word which I have spoken shall be done,* saith the Lord God.

Of course, this seemed like a direct answer, and, if it were a direct answer, it clearly meant that the prophecy of the destruction of Oakland, Alameda, and Chicago would be fulfilled at once, on the day predicted. The woman told me of this that very day, but I was not at all disturbed. As we all know, the prophecy was not fulfilled, and this would-be prophetess sank out of sight, and as far as I know has not been heard from since. Many years afterward an earthquake did come to San Francisco and work great destruction, but San Francisco was not in this woman's prophecy, and Oakland and Alameda were, and they were left practically untouched by the earthquake and certainly did not sink out of sight as the woman predicted. And furthermore, the earthquake that came to an adjoining city was many years after the prophesied date. This is only one illustration among many that might be given of how utterly misleading is any guidance that we get in this fantastic and unwarranted way.

Furthermore, the fact that some text of Scripture comes into your mind at some time when you are trying to discover God's will is not by any means proof positive that it is just the Scripture for you at that time. The devil can suggest Scripture. He did this in tempting our Lord (Matt. 4:6), and he does it today. If the text suggested, taken in its real meaning as determined by the language used and by the context, applies to your present position, it is, of course, a message from God for you, but the mere fact that a text of Scripture comes to mind at some time, which by a distortion from its proper meaning might apply to our case, is no evidence whatever that it is the guidance of God. May I repeat once more that in getting guidance from God's Word we must take the words as they are found in their connection, and interpret them according to the proper meaning of the words used and apply them to those to whom it is evident from the context that they were intended to apply. But with this word of warning against seeking God's guidance from the Word of God in fantastic and unwarranted ways, let me repeat that God's principal way of guiding us, and the way by which all other methods must be tested, is by His written Word.

II. God Leads by His Spirit

God also leads us by His Spirit, that is, by the direct leading of the Spirit in the individual heart. Beyond a question there is such a thing as an "inner light." We read in Acts 8:29, "And *the Spirit said* unto Philip, Go near and join thyself to this chariot." In a similar way we read in Acts 16:6, 7, of the apostle Paul and his companions: "And they went through the region of Phrygia and the region of Galatia, *having been forbidden of the Holy Spirit to speak* the word in Asia; and when they were come over against Mysia they assayed to go into Bithynia; and *the Spirit of Jesus suffered them not."* In one of these passages we see the Spirit of God by His Holy Spirit giving direct personal guidance to Philip as to what he should do, and in the other passage we see the Spirit restraining Paul and his companions from doing something they would otherwise have done. There is no reason why God should not lead us as directly as he led Philip and Paul in their day, and those who walk near God can testify that He does so lead. I was once walking on South Clark Street, Chicago, near the corner of Adams, a very busy corner. I had passed by hundreds of people as I walked. Suddenly I met a man, a perfect stranger, and it seemed to me as if the Spirit of God said to me, "Speak to that man." I stopped a moment and stepped into a doorway and asked God to show me if the guidance was really from Him.

It became instantly clear that it was. I turned around and followed the man, who had reached the corner and was crossing from one side of Clark street to the other. I caught up to him in the middle of the street. Providentially, for a moment there was no traffic at that point. Even on that busy street, we were alone in the middle of the street. I laid my hand upon his shoulder as we crossed to the further sidewalk, and said to him, "Are you a Christian?" He replied, "That is a strange thing to ask a perfect stranger on the street." I said, "I know it is, and I do not ask every man that I meet on the street that question, but I believe God told me to ask you." He stopped and hung his head. He said, "This is very strange. I am a graduate of Amherst College, but I am a perfect wreck through drink here in Chicago, and only yesterday my cousin, who is a minister in this city, was speaking to me about my soul, and for you, a perfect stranger, to put this question to me here on this busy street!" I did not succeed in bringing the man to a decision there on the street, but shortly afterward he was led to a definite acceptance of Christ. A friend of mine walking the busy streets of Toronto suddenly had a deep impression that he should go to the hospital and speak to someone out there. He tried to think of anyone he knew at the hospital, and he could think of but one man. He took it for granted that he was the man he was to speak to, but when he reached the hospital and came to this man's bedside there was no reason why he should speak to him, and nothing came of the conversation. He was in great perplexity, and standing by his friend's bed he asked God to guide him. He saw a man lying on the bed right across the aisle. This man was a stranger, he had been brought to the hospital for an apparently minor trouble, some difficulty with his knee. His case did not seem at all urgent, but my friend turned and spoke to him and had the joy of leading him to Christ. To everybody's surprise, that man passed into eternity that very night. It was then or never. So God often guides us today (if we are near Him and listening for His guidance) leading us to do things that we would not otherwise do, and restraining us from doing things we otherwise would do. But these inward leadings must be always tested by the Word, and we do well when any prompting comes to look up to God and ask Him to make clear to us if this leading is of Him, otherwise we may be led to do things which are absurd and not at all according to the will of God.

But though it is oftentimes our privilege to be thus led by the Spirit of God, there is *no warrant whatever in the Word of God for our refusing to act until we are thus led.* Remember *this is not God's only method of guidance.* Oftentimes we do not need this particular kind of guidance. Take the cases of Philip and of Paul to which we have referred. God did not guide Philip and Paul *in this way* in every step they took. Philip had done many things in coming down through Samaria to the desert where he met the treasurer of Queen Candace, and it was not until the chariot of the treasurer appeared that God led Philip directly by His Spirit. And so with Paul, Paul in the missionary work to which God had called him had followed his own best judgment as God enlightened it until the moment came when he needed the special direct prohibition of the Holy Spirit of his going into a place where God would not have him go at that time. There is no need for our having the Spirit's direction to do that which the Spirit has already told us to do in the Word. For example, many a man who has fanatical and unscriptural notions about the guidance of the Holy Spirit, refuses to work in an after meeting because, as he says, the Holy Spirit does not lead him to speak to anyone, and he is waiting until He does. But as the Word of God plainly teaches him to be a fisher of men (Matt. 4:19; 28:19; Acts 8:4), if he is to obey God's Word, then whenever there is opportunity to work with men he should go to work, and there is no need of the Holy Spirit's special guidance. Paul would have gone into these places to preach the gospel if the Holy Spirit had not forbidden him. He would not have waited for some direct command of the Spirit to preach, and when we have an opportunity to speak to lost souls, we should speak unless restrained. What we need is not some direct impulse of the Holy Spirit to make us speak, the Word already commands us to do that; what we need, if we are not to speak, is that the Spirit should directly forbid us to speak.

Furthermore, let me repeat again that we should bear in mind about the Spirit's guidance, that He will not lead us to do anything that is contrary to the Word of God. The Word of God is the Holy Spirit's Book, and He never contradicts His own teaching. Many people do things that are strictly forbidden in the Word of God, and justify themselves in so doing by saying the Spirit of God guides them to do it, but any spirit that guides us to do something that is contrary to the Holy Spirit's own Book cannot by any possibility be the Holy

Spirit. For example, some time ago in reasoning with one of the leaders of the Tongues Movement about the utterly unscriptural character of their assemblies, I called his attention to the fact that in the 14th chapter of 1 Corinthians we have God's explicit command that *not more than two, or at the most three*, persons should be allowed to speak "in a tongue" in any one meeting, and that *the two or three* that did speak *must not speak at the same time, but "in turn,"* and *if there were no interpreter present, not even one* should be allowed to speak in a tongue, that (while he might speak in private with himself in a tongue, even with no interpreter present) he must "keep silence in the church." I called his attention to the fact that in their assembly they disobeyed every one of these three things that God commanded. He defended himself and his companions by saying, "But we are led by the Spirit of God to do these things, and therefore are not subject to the Word." I called his attention to the fact that Word of God in this passage was given by the Holy Spirit for the specific purpose of guiding the assembly in its conduct, and that any spirit that led them to disobey these explicit commandments of the Holy Spirit Himself, given through His apostle Paul and recorded in His Word, could not by any possibility be the Holy Spirit. Here again we should always bear in mind that there are other spirits besides the Holy Spirit, and we should "try the spirits whether they be of God," and we should try them by the Word. One of the gravest mistakes that anyone can make in his Christian life is that of being so anxious for spirit guidance that he is willing to open his soul to any spirit who may come along and try to lead him.

Further still, we should always bear in mind that *there is absolutely no warrant in the Word of God for supposing that the Holy Spirit leads us in strange and absurd ways, or to do strange and absurd things.* For example, some have certain signs by which they discern, as they say, the Holy Spirit's guidance. For example, some look for a peculiar twitching of the face, or for some other physical impulse. With some the test is a shudder, or cold sensation down the back. When this comes they take it as clear evidence that the Holy Spirit is present. In a former day, and to a certain extent today, some judge the Spirit's presence by what they call "the jerks," that is, a peculiar jerking that takes possession of a person, which they suppose to be the work of the Holy Spirit. All this is absolutely unwarranted by the Word of God and dishonoring to the Holy Spirit. We are told distinctly and emphatically in 2 Timothy 1:7 that the Holy Spirit is a spirit "of power, and of love, and of a sound mind." The word translated "sound mind" really means "sound sense," and, therefore, any spirit that leads us to do ridiculous things, cannot be the Holy Spirit. There are some who defend the most outrageous improprieties and even indecencies in public assemblies, saying that the Holy Spirit prompts them to these things. By this claim they fly directly in the face of God's own Word, which teaches us specifically in 1 Corinthians 14:32, 33, that "The spirits of the prophets are subject to the prophets; for God is not a God of confusion, but of peace." And in the 40th verse we are told that "all things" in a Spirit-governed assembly should be "done decently and in order." The word translated "decently" in this passage means *"in a becoming* (or respectable) way," and this certainly does not permit the disorders and immodesties, and confusions and indecencies and absurdities that occur in many assemblies that claim to be Spirit led, but which, tested by the Word of God, certainly are not led by the *Holy Spirit.*

III. God Guides Us by Enlightening Our Judgment

In the third place God guides us by enlightening our judgment. We see an illustration of this in the case of the apostle Paul in Acts 16:10. God had been guiding Paul by a direct impression produced in his heart by the Holy Spirit, keeping him from going to certain places where he would otherwise have gone. Then God gives to Paul in the night a vision, and, having received the vision, Paul by his own enlightened judgment, concludes from it what God has called him to do. This is God's ordinary method of guidance when His Word does not specifically tell us what to do. We go to God for wisdom, we make sure that our wills are completely surrendered to Him, and that we realize our dependence upon Him for guidance, then God clears up our judgment and makes it clear to us what we should do. Here again we should always bear in mind that "God is light and in Him is no darkness at all," and that, therefore, God's guidance is clear guidance, and we should not act until things are made perfectly plain. Many miss God's guidance by doing things too soon. Had they waited until God had enabled them to see clearly, under the illumination of His Holy Spirit, they would have avoided disastrous mistakes. The principle that "he that believeth shall not make haste" (Is. 28:16) applies right here. On the other hand, when any duty is made clear we should do it at once. If we hesitate to act when the way is made clear, then we soon get into doubt and perplexity and are all at sea as to what God would have us do. Many and many a man has seen the path of duty as clear as day before him, and instead of stepping out at once, has hesitated even when the will of God has become perfectly clear, and before long he was plunged into absolute uncertainty as to what God would have him do.

IV. God May Guide by Visions and Dreams

In Acts 16:9, 10, we are told how God guided Paul by a vision, and there are other instances of such guidance not only before Pentecost, but after. God may so guide people today. However, that was not God's usual method of guiding men even in Bible times, and it is even less His usual way since the giving of the Word of God and the giving of the Holy Spirit. We do not need that mode of guidance as the Old Testament saints did, for we now have the complete Word and we also have the Spirit in a sense and in a fullness that the Old Testament saints did not. God does lead by dreams today. When I was a boy, sleeping in a room in our old home in Geneva, New York, I dreamed I was sleeping in that room and that my mother, who I dreamed was dead (though she was really living at the time) came and stood by my bed, with a face like an angel, and besought me to enter the ministry, and in my sleep I promised her that I would. In a few moments I awoke and found it all a dream, but I never could get away from that promise. I never had rest in my soul until I did give up my plans for life and promise God that I would preach. But the matter of dreams is one in which we should exercise the utmost care, and we should be very careful and prayerful and scriptural in deciding that any dream is from Him. Only the other day, a brilliant and highly-educated woman called at my office to tell me some wonderful dreams that she had and what these dreams proved. Her interpretation of the dreams was most extraordinary and fantastic. But while dreams are a very un-certain method of guidance, it will not do for us to say that God never so guides, but it is the height of folly to seek God's guidance in that way, and especially to dictate that God shall guide in that way.

V. God Does Not Guide by Casting Lots in This Dispensation

In Acts 1:24–26 we learn that the apostles sought guidance in a choice of one to take the place of Judas, by the lot. This method of finding God's will was common in the Old Testament times, but it belongs entirely to the old dispensation. This is the last case on record. It was never used after Pentecost. We need today no such crude way of ascertaining the will of God, as we have the Word and the Spirit at our disposal. Neither should we seek signs. That belongs to the imperfect dispensation that is past, and even then it was a sign of unbelief.

VI. God Guides by His Providence

God has still another way of guiding us besides those already mentioned, and that is by His providences, that is, He so shapes the events of our lives that it becomes clear that He would have us go in a certain direction or do a certain thing. For example, God puts an unsaved man directly in our way so that we are alone with him and thus have an opportunity for conversation with him. In such a case we need no vision to tell us, and we need no mighty impulse of the Holy Spirit to tell us, that we ought to speak to this man about his soul. The very fact that we are alone with him and have an opportunity for conversation is of itself all the divine guidance we need. We do need, however, to look to God to tell us what to say to him and how to say it, but God will not tell us what to say by some supernatural revelation, but by making clear to our own minds what we should say.

In a similar way if a man needs work to support himself or family, and a position for honest employment opens to him, he needs no inner voice, no direct leading of the Holy Spirit, to tell him to take the work, the opening opportunity is of itself God's guidance by God's providence.

We must, however, be very careful and very prayerful in interpreting "the leadings of providence." What some people call "the leading of providence" means no more than the easiest way. When Jonah was fleeing from God and went down to Joppa, he found a ship just ready to start for Tarshish (Jon. 1:3). If he had been like many today, he would have interpreted that as meaning it was God's will that he should go to Tarshish, as there was a ship just starting for Tarshish, instead of to Nineveh, to which city God had bidden him go. In point of fact, Jonah did take the ship to Tarshish but he was under no illusion in the matter, he knew perfectly well that he was not going where God wanted him to go, and he got into trouble for it. Oftentimes people seek guidance by providence by asking God to shut up a certain way that is opening to them, if it is not His will that they should go that way. There is no warrant whatever for doing that. God has given us our judgment and is ready to illuminate our judgment, and we have no right to act the part of children and to ask Him to shut up the way so we cannot possibly go that way if it is not His will. Some fancy that the easy way is necessarily God's way, but oftentimes the hard way is God's way. Our Lord Himself said, as recorded in Matthew 16:24, "If any man would come after me, let him deny himself, and take up his cross and follow me." That certainly is not the easy way. There are many who advise us to "follow *the path of least resistance*," but the path of least resistance is not always God's way by any means.

Some ask God to guide them providentially by removing all difficulties from the path in which He would have them go, but we have no right to offer such a prayer. God wishes us to be men and women of character and to surmount difficulties, and He oftentimes will allow difficulties to pile up in the very way in which we ought to go, and the fact that we see that a path is full of difficulties is no reason for deciding it is not the way God would have us go. Nevertheless, God does guide us by His providence, and we have no right to despise His providential guidance. For example, one may desire to go to China or to Africa as a missionary, and God does not give them the health requisite for going to China or to Africa. They should take that as clear providential guidance that they ought not to go, and seek some other opportunity of serving God.

There are many people asking God to open some door of opportunity, and God does open a door of opportunity right at hand, but it is not the kind of work they would especially like to do; so they decline to see in it a door of opportunity. The whole difficulty is that they are not wholly surrendered to the will of God.

Before we close this subject let us repeat again what cannot be emphasized too much nor too often, that all leadings, whether they be by the Spirit, by visions, by providences, by our own judgment, or advice of friends, or in any other way, must be tested by the Word of God.

The main point in the whole matter of guidance is the absolute surrender of the will to God, the delighting in His will, and the being willing to do joyfully the very things we would not like to do naturally, the very things in connection with which there may be many disagreeable circumstances, because, for example, of association with, or even subordination to those that we do not altogether like, or difficulties of other kinds, doing them joyfully, simply because it is the will of God, and the willingness to let God lead in any way He pleases, whether it be by His Word, or His Spirit, or by the enlightening of our judgment, or by His providence, or whatever way He will. If we will only completely distrust our own judgment and have absolute confidence in God's judgment and God's willingness to guide us, and are absolutely surrendered to His will, whatever it may be, and are willing to let God choose His way of guidance, and will go on step by step as He does guide us, and if we are daily studying His Word to know His will, and are listening for the still small voice of the Spirit, going step by step as He leads, He will guide us with His eye; He will guide us with His counsel to the end of our earthly pilgrimage, and afterwards receive us into glory.

Study Questions

1. In what ways does God guide?
2. Why is surrendering to the will of God important when seeking His guidance?

13

God's Keeping and How to Make Sure of It

O ur subject this morning is God's keeping and how to make sure of it. How to enjoy or make sure of God's keeping will come out when we come to a consideration of whom God keeps. The Bible, both the Old and New Testaments, is full of passages on this important subject of God's keeping, and we shall look at quite a number of these passages this morning, but no one of them can properly be considered the text of the entire sermon. I am going to give you a Bible reading rather than a sermon. Let us look first at John 17:11 (This comes nearer being the text of the whole sermon than any other), "And I am no more in the world, and these are in the world, and I come to Thee. Holy Father, keep them in the name which Thou hast given me, that they may be one even as we are." This was Jesus' prayer. I am glad He offered it; for the Father heareth Him always, and I am sure of God's keeping because the Lord Jesus asked that I might be kept. Most wonderfully does this prayer of our Lord and Savior bring out the security of those who belong to Him. In the next verse He goes on to say that while He was with His disciples He kept them in the Father's name. Yes, He says more than that, He says, "I guarded them, *and not one* of them perished." The son of perdition perished, and he was one of the apostolic company, but he was never really one of those who belonged to Christ, he was not one of those whom the Father had given to Jesus Christ. Christ Himself declares that Judas was a devil from the beginning (John 6:70). But now our Lord was leaving His disciples, and He turned their keeping over to the Father, and it is now the Father who keeps us, and it is this keeping which we are to study this morning. What the Bible tells us of God's keeping can be classified under five main headings:(1) Whom God Keeps; (2) What He Keeps; (3) From What He Keeps; (4) How He Keeps; (5) Unto What He Keeps.

I. Whom God Keeps

We look first at whom God keeps, and by discovering that we will discover how any one of us may be sure of His glorious keeping.

1. Whom He keeps we are told in the very verse that we have just been reading, John 17:11, 12. Here the Lord Jesus prays to the Father to keep those whom the Father Himself hath given to Christ, and says that He himself during His earthly life had kept these whom His Father had given Him. *Those whom God keeps then are those who belong to Christ, those whom the Father has given to Him.* The clear teaching of these verses is that there is a body of persons who belonged in a peculiar way to God, and whom God gave to His Son. This company of people, and their security and privileges, are frequently mentioned in the gospel of John. Those whom God keeps are those who belong to this company. The way then to be sure of God's keeping is to make sure that we belong to this company whom the Father has given to Christ. But who are these, and how can any one of us tell whether or not we belong to this privileged company.

(1) This question is answered in John 6:37 where Jesus is recorded as saying, "All that which the Father giveth me shall come unto me; and him that cometh to me I will in no wise cast out." From this it is clear that *all those who come to Christ belong to that elect company whom the Father has given unto Him.* Every man who really comes to Christ, comes to Him as his Savior, as his Master, as his Lord, and commits himself unreservedly to Him, for Christ to save and to rule, he is one of those whom God has given to Christ, and whom God therefore keeps. Are you one of this number? Have you come to Christ in this real way? If you are, God will keep you. If not, will you come to Christ today and thus make sure that you will be kept?

(2) We have still another description of those whom God has given to Christ, in John 17:6, He says, "I manifested Thy name unto the men whom Thou gavest me out of the world: Thine they were and Thou gavest them to me; and *they have kept Thy Word.*" Here we are told that those whom the Father gave to the Son were

those who kept God's Word. Everyone who keeps God's Word may be sure that he belongs to the elect company whom God the Father Himself will keep. Notice carefully Christ's description of them: "they have *kept* Thy Word." That is to say, they not only hear God's Word, not only obey it, they *keep* God's Word, that is, they treasure it, they regard it as their most precious treasure, and they will not give it up for any gain that may be offered them in place of it. These are those whom God keeps. *If we keep God's Words, God Himself will keep us.* Are you keeping God's words?

2. Isaiah 26:3 also tells us whom God keeps. Here the prophet says in speaking to God, "Thou wilt keep him in perfect peace, *whose mind is stayed on Thee:* because he trusteth in Thee." *God keeps the one whose mind is stayed upon Him, the one who looks not at self but at God, looks not at circumstances, but at God; the one who puts confidence in God.* The keeping of this passage is a different one from that which is spoken of in John 17. There it is a keeping from perishing, here it is a keeping from all anxiety and worry. We shall see this more clearly when we come to speak of from what God keeps us.

II. What God Keeps

Now let us look at what God keeps. Paul tells us in 2 Timothy 1:12 just what God keeps. He says, "I know whom I have believed, and am persuaded that He is able to keep (guard) that which I have committed unto Him against that day." The word translated "keep" in this passage in the Revised Version is rendered "guard," but it is the same word that is used in John 17:2, though not the same word that is used in John 17:11. Here we are taught that *God keeps (or guards) that which is committed unto Him.* Some commit more unto God, some less, but what is committed unto Him He keeps. Some commit the keeping of their souls unto God (1 Pet. 4:19), some commit their temporal affairs unto Him, some commit their health unto Him, some more, some less, but whatever is committed to Him He keeps. Dorothea Trudel, a German woman, tells how her mother was a woman of great faith in prayer, and though her father was a drinking man who made little or no provision for the family, and the children numbered eleven, and their straits were sometimes great, they always were saved from suffering. She says:

There were times when we had not a farthing left in the house. None but God knew of our condition, and He who feedeth the young ravens when they cry was not unmindful of the petitions of His faithful child. He ever helped us in our time of need. It was on this account that our mother's favorite motto, "Pray, but do not beg," has been so impressed upon our minds. When one of the children was asked on what her mother relied in her poverty, the child said, "On God alone. She never tells us how God is going to help, but she is always certain His aid will come at the right time."

The experience of this German woman could be duplicated in the experience of thousands in our own land and other lands. It was related of Mrs. Jane C. Pithey, a member of the Centenary Methodist Church in Chicago, that for years she was disabled by the shaking palsy and received all her supplies in answer to prayer. When her husband died he left in his pocketbook two silver quarters. Besides the little cottage, this was all that she had to support herself and a bedridden mother of nearly ninety years of age. It is said:

she went to God in prayer and day by day each want was met. Each needed article was asked for by name until her hired girl was astounded at the constant answers given. One morning as Mrs. Pithey was rising from her knees at the family worship, the girl burst out, 'You have forgotten to pray for coal and we are entirely out.' So, as she stood, she added a petition for the coal. About an hour after, the bell rang, she went to the door and there was a load of coal sent by a man who knew nothing of her want, and who had never sent anything before, nor ever has since.

Many other instances are related regarding her of God's keeping and supplying all her needs. Some commit their work to God, some commit everything. His keeping will be just in proportion to our committing.

II. From What God Keeps

1. First of all, *God keeps those who belong to His Son Jesus Christ from perishing.* This comes out very plainly in the passage with which we started, John 17:11, 12. Our Lord prayed, "Holy Father, keep them in Thy name, which Thou hast given me, that they may be one even as we are." Then He goes on to say, "While I was with them, I kept them in Thy name which Thou hast given me: and I guarded them, and *not one of them perished,* but the son of perdition." The one who truly

comes to Christ, the one who enters with his whole heart in the fellowship of Christ, the one who fully receives Christ as his Savior from the guilt and power of sin, the one who wholeheartedly and unreservedly surrenders to Christ as his Master, God keeps from ever perishing. No matter how numerous, how subtle, how mighty the assaults of Satan, of sin, and of error may be, God will keep him. As the Lord Jesus puts it in another place (John 10:28, 29), "I give unto them eternal life; and they shall never perish, and no one shall snatch them out of my hand. My Father which hath given them unto me, is greater than all and no one is able to snatch them out of the Father's hand." This is the position of the one who belongs to Christ, the almighty hand of Jesus Christ the Son underneath him, the almighty hand of God the Father over him, and there he is, in between those two almighty hands, perfectly sheltered, and no person and no power in heaven or earth or hell can ever get him.

2. But it is not only from perishing that God keeps us, *He also keeps us from falling.* As we read in Jude 24, He "is able to keep us from falling and to present us faultless before the presence of His glory with exceeding joy." The word translated "falling" in this passage is translated "stumbling" in the Revised Version and this is the exact force of the word. One may fall without perishing, but one need not even fall, indeed he need not even stumble. God can keep us from even this, and will keep us from this if we look to Him and trust Him to do it. But when we get our eyes off of Him down we go, but He still keeps us from perishing. He sees to it that we get up again even if we do stumble. Though we stumble we are still kept, just as Peter was, from making utter shipwreck. Peter was in Satan's sieve, but nevertheless he was still kept by God in answer to Christ's intercessory prayer, and Christ always lives to make intercession for us and so "is able to save *to the uttermost*" (Heb. 7:25). What comfort there is in this verse to the one who hesitates to begin the Christian life because he knows his weakness and is afraid that he will stumble and fall. If you will only put yourself wholly in God's hands, He is able, no matter how weak you may be in yourself, to keep you even from stumbling.

3. But it is not only from perishing and from stumbling that God keeps, *He keeps the one whose mind is stayed upon Him in perfect peace.* This glad gospel we find in that book in the Old Testament which is so full of the gospel, the prophecy of Isaiah. We read in Isaiah 26:3,

"Thou wilt keep him in perfect peace, whose mind is stayed on Thee: because he trusteth in Thee." Then Isaiah goes on to say, "Trust ye in the Lord forever: for in the Lord Jehovah is everlasting strength." God keeps from all anxiety those who may stay their minds upon Him. If we will only take our eyes off of ourselves and off of men, and off of circumstances, and stay our minds upon God and upon Him alone and upon His sure promises, He will keep us in perfect peace. These are precious words for such a time as that in which we live, where one does not know any morning when he takes up his paper what he may read. No matter how perilous our position may seem, no matter how unlooked for and how unwelcome our surroundings may be, if we stay our minds upon the Lord Jehovah, He will keep us in perfect peace. We have an illustration of this in Caleb and Joshua in the Old Testament (Num. 13:17, 26, 28–30; 14:1, 3, 7–9). The ten spies that accompanied Caleb and Joshua into the land looked at circumstances and were filled with dismay. Caleb and Joshua looked away from circumstances, they looked right over the heads of the giants, they looked at God and His Word. They stayed their minds on Him and He kept them in perfect peace. It was so with Paul also in the awful storm and impending shipwreck on the Mediterranean. The crew and soldiers were cowering with fear as they heard the howling of the wind and saw the fierceness and force of the dashing waves, but Paul looked over the waves and over the storm at God and His Word, and stayed His mind on Him, and God kept Him in perfect peace so that Paul could say to his cowering companions, "Sirs, be of good cheer: for I *believe* God that it shall be even so as it has been spoken unto me" (Acts 27:25). Oh, we need men and women of just such imperturbable calm as that in such days of stress and storm as those in which we are now living. If we would only stay our minds upon God, if we would only really trust Him, if we would only really believe His Word that it will *be even as it has been told us,* we would never have a single ruffle of anxiety. There is one passage in the Word of God which taken alone would be able, if we would only bear it in mind and believe it, to banish all fears and all anxiety forever, that passage is Romans 8:28, "We know that all things work together for good to them that love God, to them who are the called according to His purpose." Whatever comes to us must be one of the "all things" and if we believed this passage we would know that however threatening it may appear, and however bad in itself it may really be, that it must work together with the other things that God sends into our lives, for our highest good. How then can we ever have a moment's worry?

IV. How God Keeps

Now let us turn to the question of how God keeps.

1. We are told in Deuteronomy 32:9, 10, that *Jehovah keeps His people "as the apple of His eye."* The eye is the most wonderfully protected portion of the body, and "the apple" or pupil of the eye is the most important part of the eye, the lens, and is especially provided for and protected. The mechanism of the eye and the provision for its welfare that God has made has always awakened the wonder and admiration of men of science. It is shielded and guarded in every conceivable way, and just so God guards His people with the utmost care, with every conceivable and inconceivable safeguard against their injury. Each year brings into view some new provision God has made for our safety.

2. We are taught in Genesis 28:15 that *God keeps those who trust and obey Him "in all places whereever" they go.* He kept Joseph in his father's house; He kept him in the pit in the wilderness; He kept him in Potiphar's house; He kept him in the Egyptian prison; He kept him in the palace. God kept David from the fury and power of the lion and the bear as he watched the sheep in the wilderness; He kept him in security through all the years that Saul hunted him like a partridge in the mountains (1 Sam. 26:20); He kept him in the face of the many foes that arose against him when he became king; He kept him everywhere, so that David could write, "Yea, though I walk through the valley of the shadow of death, I will fear no evil, for thou art with me." And so God keeps us if we trust and obey Him, *in all places whereever we go.*

3. In Psalm 121:3, 4 we are taught *God keeps His people at all times.* He that keeps us never "slumbers nor sleeps." We are not only kept in all places, but also at all times. God is never off guard, He never sleeps at His post. Satan can never catch one of God's children when their watchman is sleeping. I am glad of this. You and I are often off guard. Satan can often catch us napping, but he can never catch us when our Watchman is napping.

4. But there is another thought about God's keeping which, if possible, is even more precious, and that is *He keeps to all eternity*. Here again we think of John 10:28, "I give unto them eternal life: and they shall *never perish*, and no one shall snatch them out of my hand." Those who trust in Christ shall *"never perish."* This is one of the most precious facts about God's keeping, *it never ends*. We may prove unfaithful, but He ever abideth faithful, He cannot deny Himself (2 Tim. 2:13). He keepeth to the end. We shall never perish, or, to translate more literally as well as more expressively, "in no wise (shall we) perish, forever." We stand today and look forward into the never-ending future. If we know ourselves well and look at ourselves alone, we may well tremble at the thought of how utterly we may fail some time in those ever rolling years; but, if we look up to God and know Him, we will not tremble, for *He* never faileth, and we have His Word for it that He will ever keep us. He keeps me today "as the apple of His eye," He will keep me in all places, He will keep me at all times, He will keep me to all eternity.

V. Unto What God Keeps

We have seen whom God keeps; we have seen what God keeps; we have seen from what God keeps; we have seen how God keeps, one thought remains, *unto what does God keep*. This question is answered in 1 Peter 1:5, We *"are kept by the power of God unto a salvation ready to be revealed in the last time."* Upon this we have no time to dwell. Simply let me say this, that the salvation that we have today, no matter how complete it may seem, even though we know not only the forgiveness of sins and adoption into the family of God, but also deliverance from sin's power, a life of daily victory, is not the whole of salvation. Completed salvation lies in the eternal future. It includes not merely the salvation of the spirit and the soul, it includes the salvation of the body, that "salvation ready to be revealed in the last times," is the salvation that we shall possess when the wondrous promises about our being transformed into the perfect likeness of Jesus Christ, not only spiritually and morally and mentally, but also physically, have their fulfillment, and unto that salvation God keeps us.

Beloved fellow believer in God and in Jesus Christ His Son, have you realized fully what God's keeping means? Have you enjoyed the security that is yours, and the rest of mind that might be yours? Have you put as much into His hands to keep as He is willing to keep? Are you letting Him keep you in perfect peace in the midst of the trial and uncertainty and travail and turmoil and storm and stress of these trying days? If not, will you do it today?

And friends, you who are not Christians, do you not see how precious a thing God's keeping is? Is it not immeasurably better than anything this world has to give? Some trust in riches, some in their own abilities, some in powerful friends, some in national leaders and "preparedness," but better, infinitely better to trust in God, for "He will keep him in perfect peace whose mind is stayed upon Him, because he trusteth in Him." Will you not put your trust in Him and have a share in this wondrous prayer of the Savior, "Holy Father, keep through Thine own name those whom Thou hast given me."

Study Questions

1. Whom does God "keep"?
2. What does Isaiah 26:3 say?
3. What does God keep?
4. What does God keep us from?
5. How does God keep us?
6. What does God keep us for?

14

The Complete and Symmetrical Life, and How to Attain to It

But the fruit of the Spirit is love, joy, peace, longsuffering, gentleness (kindness), goodness, faith (faithfulness), meekness, temperance (Gal. 5:22, 23).

The average life is a very partial life. Even the life of the average Christian is a very partial life, a one-sided life, it is a life in which there is much lacking. There may be many admirable things about it, but there is a deplorable lack of other things—the life is incomplete, it is devoid of balance and symmetry, strong in some directions, perhaps amazingly strong in those directions, but lacking, perhaps amazingly lacking in other directions. It is like an imperfect rose, perfectly formed and beautifully tinted in one part, but blasted and withered in another part. What each one of us needs is a full life, a well-rounded life, a well-balanced life, a symmetrical life. There is a passage in the Word of God that wonderfully pictures such a life, complete in all its parts and symmetrical in its every detail. This passage not only pictures this life, but tells us how to attain to it. The passage is Galatians 5:22, "But the fruit of the Spirit is love, joy, peace, longsuffering, gentleness, goodness, faith, meekness, temperance." Some years ago during attendance at a Bible Conference in St. Louis, I was entertained at a private home. When I awoke in the morning the first thing that I saw as I opened my eyes was these words looped around the room in large and beautifully colored letters, "The fruit of the Spirit is love, joy, peace, longsuffering, gentleness, goodness,

131

faith, meekness, temperance." They brought a blessing to my heart that morning and set me to thinking deeply upon the words. From that day to this I have had a longing to preach on this text but have never done it until this hour. The text presents to us two main thoughts, the complete and symmetrical life described, and how to attain to this complete and symmetrical life.

I. The Complete and Symmetrical Life Described

1. The first characteristic in this life is "LOVE." "The fruit of the Spirit is love." Paul does not say whether he has in mind love to God or love to man, he just says "LOVE," without definition as to its objects, so love as here spoken of includes all objects. The complete life is characterized by love to both God and man, and love to all classes and conditions of men. It obeys the first and great commandment, "Thou shalt love the Lord thy God, with all thy heart, and with all thy soul, and with all thy mind," and it also obeys the second command, "Thou shalt love thy neighbor as thyself." Yes, it goes beyond the second commandment and obeys the new commandment which the Lord gave to His disciples, that they love one another, even as He loved us (John 13:34). In moral attributes, "love" is the one preeminently divine thing, "God is love" (1 John 4:8). If love is lacking, all else counts for nothing, and the life is not only incomplete, it is worthless.

If I speak with the tongues of men and of angels, but have not love, I am become sounding brass, or a clanging cymbal. And if I have the gift of prophecy, and know all mysteries and all knowledge; and if I have all faith, so as to remove mountains, but have not love, I am nothing. And if I bestow all my goods to feed the poor, and though I give my body to be burned, and have not love, it profiteth me nothing (1 Cor. 13:1–3).

"The old time religion," as the song goes, "makes me love everybody," and the complete life is the life of the one who "*loves everybody.*" There is absolutely no man whom the Spirit-filled man does not love. No matter how grievously one may have wronged us, no matter how grossly they may have slandered us, no matter how gravely they have injured us, if we are filled with the Spirit, we will love them.

2. But while "LOVE" is the first thing and the supreme thing in the complete life, it is not the only thing. Following "LOVE" comes "JOY." "The fruit of the Spirit is love, joy." A life that is not a radiantly joy-

ful life is an incomplete life and unsymmetrical life, it is lacking in one of the principal elements that go to make up the complete life, it is not a life after God's pattern. Even if our lives were given up wholly to serving God and our fellowmen with utter devotion and utter forgetfulness of self, if they were not joyful lives, they would dishonor God. Jesus was called upon to be a propitiation for sins, to be a substitute Savior, to take our sins and their penalty upon Himself, and He was, therefore, "a man of sorrows and acquainted with grief," nevertheless, He was a joy-full man. On the night before His crucifixion, only an hour or so before the agonies of Gethsemane, He said, "These things have I spoken unto you, that my joy may be in you, and that your joy may be filled full" (John 15:11). To have His joy then is to have fullness of joy, and, if our joy is to be *"filled full"* by having His joy, He must Himself have been a joy-full man. Constant joy is the commanded duty as well as the promised privilege of a child of God, a believer in the Lord Jesus Christ. "Rejoice in the Lord always," the Holy Spirit commands us in Philippians 4:4, then adds, "again I say, Rejoice." When Paul wrote these words he was a prisoner under most distressing circumstances, and awaiting possible sentence of execution, yet the whole epistle that he wrote is jubilant from start to finish. The Spirit-filled life will always be joyful and jubilant, nothing can disturb its joy. No matter how adverse its circumstances, its joy abideth; for its joy is not in circumstances but in Him who is the same yesterday, today, and forever. The Holy Spirit is called, in Hebrews 1:9, "The oil of gladness," and when God pours out His Holy Spirit upon us, "He anoints us with the oil of gladness," and the oil of gladness flows down over us and suffuses the whole person.

3. But even "LOVE" and "JOY" together, wonderful as they are, do not constitute all that there is of the complete and symmetrical life. Following "LOVE" and "JOY" comes "PEACE." "The fruit of the Spirit is love, joy, peace." Paul does not say whether he means peace in our own hearts or peace with others. The reason that he does not say which he means is because he means both. The Holy Spirit brings peace into the heart in which He rules, and He brings peace with others to the one in whose heart He rules. In the verse almost immediately following the command to "rejoice always," the Spirit of God goes on to say, "In nothing be anxious; but in everything by prayer and supplication, with thanksgiving, let your requests be made known unto

God. *And the peace of God, which passeth all understanding, shall guard your hearts and your thoughts in Christ Jesus"* (Phil. 4:6, 7). Oh, how wonderful is the deep, serene, unruffled peace with which the Holy Spirit fills the heart. Some years ago a minister at a Bible Conference at Grove City came to me and said, "Two young men, college students, from my church were at the Northfield Conference this summer, and when they returned from the Conference they called on me and said, 'Pastor, we think we have heard of something that you do not know.'" This was a rather presumptuous thing for two young college students to say to a pastor over sixty years of age who was well known for his knowledge of the Word of God and the faithfulness of his ministry, but the minister showed the real depth of his earnestness and spirituality by his reply. He said, "Well, young men, if you have something good that I haven't I want to know about it." The pastor continued, "They told me of an address they had heard on the baptism with the Holy Spirit, and how the baptism with the Holy Spirit was to be obtained. When they left my study," the pastor continued,

I took my hat and went out into the woods and sat down upon a log that had fallen and thought over what they had said, and then I looked up to God and I said, Oh, God, if these young men have something that I have not, I want it. Now, oh, God, the best I know how, I absolutely surrender my will to Thee, to be whatever thou wishest me to be, to go wherever thou wishest me to go, to do whatever thou wishest me to do. Immediately after I had done this [he continued], there came into my heart such a wonderful peace and rest as I had never known.

What was the explanation? The pastor had fulfilled the conditions of receiving the Holy Spirit and He had come to do His work, and part of His fruit is "PEACE." But the Holy Spirit brings us into peace with others as well as bringing peace into us. He saves us from contentiousness. I knew a man who was naturally a man of war, he was a born fighter; he delighted in a scrap from early boyhood as in almost nothing else, but the Spirit of God got control of his life, and in so far as the Holy Spirit did gain control of his life he became a man of peace. Many and many a time he was able to keep peace under most aggravating circumstances without even a struggle. Yes, the Holy Spirit brings peace between men, especially peace between brethren. This is the immediate thought of the context in which we find our text. Going back in the chapter to the 14th and 15th verses, we read, "For the whole law is fulfilled in one word, even in this: Thou shalt love thy neighbor as thyself. But if ye *bite and devour one another,* take heed that ye be not consumed one of another." Then going down to the 19th verse we read,

Now the works of the flesh are manifest, which are these: fornication, uncleanness, lasciviousness, idolatry, sorcery, enmities, strife, jealousies, wraths, factions, divisions, parties, envyings, drunkenness, revelings, and such like; of which I forewarn you, even as I did forewarn you, that they who practice such things shall not inherit the kingdom of God.

Then comes our text, "The fruit of the Spirit is love, joy, peace, and so forth." Two lives are placed in vivid contrast to one another, the life of the flesh, full of contention and strife and quarreling, and the life in the Spirit, full of peace, longsuffering, and so forth. The perfect man keeps out of war, even under great provocation. As the Holy Spirit puts it through the apostle James in James 3:14–18, "But if ye have bitter jealousy and faction in your heart, glory not and lie not against the truth. This wisdom is not a wisdom that cometh down from above, but is earthly sensual, devilish. For where jealousy and faction are, there is confusion and every vile deed. But the wisdom that is from above is first pure, then *peaceable, gentle, easy to be entreated, full of mercy* and good fruits, *without variance,* without hypocrisy. And the fruit of righteousness is sown *in peace* for them that make peace." Oh, that the Holy Spirit ruled among nations as well as in individuals today, the war would end in five minutes, and when the Holy Spirit rules in a church, church quarrels cease instantly.

4. But "LOVE," "JOY," "PEACE," as beautiful as they are, do not constitute the whole of the complete and symmetrical life. Following "LOVE," "JOY," and "PEACE" come "LONGSUFFERING." "The fruit of the Spirit is love, joy, peace, longsuffering." This fourth characteristic of the complete and symmetrical life, the Spirit-filled life, is closely connected with the third. The truly strong man does not quickly resent injuries done by others. He is never suspicious nor sensitive. No matter how great and strong a man may be in other respects, if he is quick to resent the insult or injury which is not imaginary but very real, he is not a truly strong man, and he surely is not a Spirit-governed man, he is governed by the flesh and not by the

Spirit. Oh, how beautiful is the attitude of longsuffering in an individual or a nation, what a mark it is of real strength. The nation that is not quick to take umbrage nor "defend its honor" is not dishonored, but great and strong.

5. The fifth characteristic of the complete and symmetrical life is "GENTLENESS." "The fruit of the Spirit is love, joy, peace, longsuffering, gentleness." The primary meaning of the adjective from which the noun translated "gentleness" is derived is "fit for use," or "useful," then it comes to mean "mild," "pleasant," as opposed to "harsh," "hard," "sharp," "bitter." Then it comes to mean "gentle," "pleasant," "kind," "benevolent," "benign." How beautiful it is when a great man is also a *gentle* man, a gentleman in the true sense, a kindly man. The great example of gentleness or kindness is Jesus Himself. So many leading men in the church in our day, gifted men, go pushing through the common crowd regardless of the slow and dull, regardless of whose toes they step on; they are brusque and pushing. Not so was Jesus, "The bruised reed" He would "not break" and "the smoking flax" He would "not quench," and not so is the Spirit-filled man, he is "kindly." The Revised Version translated the word here "kindness" but I like "kindliness" better than either "gentleness" or "kindness." Are you a kindly man? Jesus was. Are you a kindly woman? If not, you have not entered into the complete and symmetrical life, not yet.

6. The sixth characteristic of the complete and symmetrical life is "GOODNESS." "The fruit of the Spirit is love, joy, peace, longsuffering, gentleness, goodness." The word so translated is a word of wide meaning and is difficult of exact definition, but the thought here, as determined by the setting, is that attribute that leads men to be always looking for and improving opportunities for doing any kind of good to anybody and everybody, in every possible place, and at every possible time. The tenth verse of the following chapter gives the thought, "So then, as we have opportunity, let us work that which is good toward all men."

7. The seventh characteristic of the complete and symmetrical life is "FAITH." "The fruit of the Spirit is love, joy, peace, longsuffering, gentleness, goodness, faith." The Revised Version reads "faithfulness," but without any warrant whatever either in usage or context. The word is the same word which is translated "faith" 238 times out of the 242 times that it is used in the New Testament, and in the four re-

maining instances it is translated "belief" or "believe," and never once is it translated "faithfulness." True faith will inevitably lead to faithfulness, and thus implies faithfulness, but "faith" is what Paul wrote, or rather the Holy Ghost wrote through Paul, and the Holy Ghost meant just what He wrote. A life without "FAITH," faith in God and faith in the Lord Jesus Christ, is a sadly incomplete and altogether unsymmetrical life. The Holy Spirit begets simple, childlike, imperturbable faith in the heart He rules, faith in God, faith in Jesus Christ, faith in the Word of God. Jesus says in John 7:17, "If any man willeth to do His (God's) will, he shall know of the teaching, whether it be of God, or whether I speak from myself." He here makes *obedience* the condition of faith in the Word of God, but in Acts 5:32 we are told that God gives the Holy Spirit to them that *obey* Him. Oh, when a man submits his life to the absolute control of the Holy Spirit, his whole thought and feeling and will are illuminated with faith, and because he has faith in God and faith in God's Word he has great expectations, he is never discouraged, he is never pessimistic, never despondent, he marches forth confidently every day to victory. He is sure he will win, and win he will.

8. The eighth characteristic of the complete and symmetrical life is "MEEKNESS." "The fruit of the Spirit is love, joy, peace, longsuffering, gentleness, goodness, faith, meekness." The exact meaning of the word rendered "meekness" in this passage is that attitude of mind that is opposed to harshness and contentiousness, and that shows itself in gentleness and tenderness in dealing with others. The man who has attained to the complete life is never harsh. Stern and severe he may sometimes have to be out of regard to the best interests of the offender himself, but his sternness and severity are aflame with gentleness. Read the first verse of the next chapter and you will get the exact thought, "Brethren, even if a man be overtaken in any trespass (the thought is of a man caught in the act of wrong-doing, wrong-doing even of the grossest kind), ye which are spiritual, restore such a one *in a spirit of meekness;* looking to thyself, lest thou also be tempted."

9. The ninth and last characteristic of the complete and symmetrical life is "TEMPERANCE." "The fruit of the Spirit is love, joy, peace, longsuffering, gentleness, goodness, faith, meekness, temperance." The Revised Version says "SELF-CONTROL," and that gives the thought, though it is not really *self*-control, but Holy Spirit control,

but it is self that is controlled. It does not mean temperance in the narrow sense we have given it in modern parlance, as applying to only one kind of excess, excess in alcoholic drinks, it means mastery of self along all lines. The highest form of mastery in the world is self-mastery. "He that ruleth his spirit is better than he that taketh a city" (Prov. 16:32). This then is the complete life, a life manifesting love, joy, peace, longsuffering, kindliness, goodness, faith, meekness, self-mastery. You will note that our text says that these things are "the *fruit* of the Spirit," not the *fruits* of the Spirit. They are the many delicious flavors of the one fruit. Wherever the Holy Spirit is given control, not some, but all of these will be seen.

II. How to Obtain the Complete and Symmetrical Life

We come now to the very practical question how to obtain this life, or how to attain to it. We have but a few minutes to answer the question, and we need but a few minutes. The verse makes the way of attainment as clear as day. We are told that these things are *"the fruit of the Spirit."* They are set over against "the works of the flesh" described in the verses that immediately precede. In other words, the things described under "the works of the flesh" are the things that are natural to us, these things are what the Holy Spirit works supernaturally in us. They are the fruit the Holy Spirit bears in us, and all that we need to do is to come to the end of ourselves and realize our own utter inability to attain to the complete and symmetrical life here pictured, and having first received the Lord Jesus Christ as our Savior, and through receiving Him as our Savior, having received the Holy Spirit to dwell in us (for He does dwell in every believer), just surrender the entire control of our lives to His dominion for Him to work in us what He will, and when the Holy Spirit is thus given complete control, the result will be that His fruit will appear on the tree of our own lives. There will be love, joy, peace, longsuffering, kindliness, goodness, faith, meekness, self-control. Wonderful indeed is the privilege of the Spirit-filled life. Will you today give up your fruitless struggles after holiness, your self efforts to lead a "life well pleasing to God," come to the end of yourself and realizing that in you, that is, in your flesh, dwelleth no good thing, surrender your whole life to the control of the Holy Spirit, then on your life will hang this "sun-kist" fruit, "love, joy, peace, longsuffering, kindliness, faith, meekness, self-mastery."

Study Questions

1. What are the fruit of the Spirit, and how evident are those fruit in your own life?
2, Who bears the fruit in us, and how do we obtain this "sun-kist" fruit?

15

The Secret of Blessedness in Heart, Beauty in Character, Fruitfulness in Service, and Prosperity in Everything

Blessed is the man that walketh not in the counsel of the ungodly, nor standeth in the way of sinners, nor sitteth in the seat of the scornful. But his delight is in the law of the Lord; and in his law doth he meditate day and night. And he shall be like a tree planted by the rivers of water, that bringeth forth his fruit in his season; his leaf also shall not wither; and whatsoever he doeth shall prosper (Ps. 1:1–3).

In these verses, God speaking through the Psalmist sets before us the secret of blessedness in heart, beauty in character, fruitfulness in service, and prosperity in everything. Are not these the four things that we all desire for ourselves? These verses tell us in the plainest sort of way how we may obtain them. They tell us that if we will not do three things and will do two things, we shall have blessedness in our hearts, beauty in our characters, fruitfulness in our service, and prosperity in whatsoever we do.

I. The Three Things We Must Not Do

The three things that we must not do are, First, Walk in the counsel of the ungodly; second, Stand in the way of sinners; third, Sit in the seat of the scornful, that is, we must come out from the world and be separate in our walk, we must not walk in the counsel of the ungodly; we must get our directions as to our walk from God and not from the world. We must not ask what the world does or advises, we must ask what God tells us to do. As to our standing, it must not be in the way of sinners; as to our sitting, or continuous fellowship, it must not be in the seat of the scornful. We will not dwell on these three things that we must not do for the words are so plain as to need no comment; what they need is not so much to be expounded as to be obeyed; and furthermore, if we do the two things which we must do, we will be sure not to do the three things which we must not do.

II. The Two Things Which We Must Do

The first of the two things which we must do is *"Delight in the law of the Lord."* The law of the Lord is God's will as revealed in His Word and these words tell us that it is not enough merely to read God's Word; indeed, that it is not enough even to earnestly study God's Word, we must *delight* in God's Word. We must have greater joy in the Word of God than in any other book, or in all other books put together. Now doubtless many of us will have to admit that we do not delight in the law of the Lord. Probably we read it, quite likely we study it diligently, but we read it and study it simply because we think it is our duty. As to delighting in it, we do not. If many of you were to reveal the exact facts about yourself, you would have to say, "I would rather read the newspaper than the Word of God. I would rather read the latest novel than the Word of God." When I was thirteen years of age, I was told that if I read three chapters in the Bible every week-day and five every Sunday, I would read the Bible in a year, and I started out to do it, and I have read the Bible every day of my life from that time to this, but for years I did not delight in it. I read it simply because I thought I ought to, or because I was uneasy if I did not, but as for delighting in it, it was the dullest, most stupid book in the world to me. I would rather have read last year's almanac than the Bible. And what was true of me then, and remained true for years, is true of many a professed Christian today. They may study the Bible every day but simply do it from a sense of duty or because their conscience is uneasy if they do not.

What shall one do if he does not delight in the law of the Lord? The answer is very simple.

(1) First of all, he must be born-again. The one who is truly born-again will love the Word of God. The Lord Jesus says in John

8:47, "He that is of God heareth God's words: Ye therefore hear them not, because ye are not of God." The little Greek word which is translated "*of*" in this passage is a very significant word. It really means and should be translated "out of," that is, in this connection "born of"; and what Jesus said was that the one that was born of God would have an ear for God's word, and that the reason that the Jews did not really have an ear for God's Word was because they were not born of God. One of the clearest proofs that a man is born of God is that he loves, *delights in* God's Word. I have seen men and women pass in a moment from an utter distaste for God's Word to an abounding delight in God's Word by simply being born-again.

"But," someone will say, "how may I be born again?" God Himself answers the question in a very simple way in John 1:12. "But as many as RECEIVED HIM, to them gave He power to become the sons of God, even to them that believe on His name." According to these words the way to be born-again is by simply *receiving Him*, receiving the Lord Jesus. The moment any man, woman, or child really receives Jesus to be to themselves all that He offers Himself to be to anyone, to be their Savior from the guilt of sin by His death upon the cross, to be their Savior from the power of sin, by His resurrection power (Heb. 7:25) and to be their Lord and Master, to whom they surrender the entire control of their lives (Acts 2:36), that moment that man, woman or child is born-again with the new life thus obtained they will get a new love, a love for God and a delight in His Word.

(2) In the second place, *in order to delight in the law of the Lord we must feed upon it.* Jeremiah says in Jeremiah 15:16, "Thy words were found, and I did *eat* them; and thy word was unto me the joy and rejoicing of mine heart." The reason why many do not delight in the Word of God is because they do not eat it. They read it; they skim over it, they smell of it, but they do not eat it, and yet they wonder why they do not delight in God's Word. What would you think if some day some friend came to visit you who had never eaten strawberries, and you should get for him a dish of our wonderful California strawberries. You tell him how delicious they are and set them before him—you are called away but in an hour or two you come back and you say to your friend, "How did you like those strawberries?" He replies, "I did not care for them. I have seen many things that I have enjoyed more." In surprise you say, "What, did not care for them?"

"No, they seemed very ordinary to me." For a moment you are puzzled, and then you say to him, "Did you eat the berries?" "No," he answers, "I did not eat them. I smelled of them and I have smelled many things that smell better." Well, that is the way that many, even of professing Christians treat the Word of God. They just smell of it, they skim over a few verses, or many verses, or many chapters, but they do not stop to eat a single verse. They do not chew the words, swallow them and assimilate them. Oh, how different the Word of God becomes when we really *eat* it. Take for example, the most familiar passage in the Bible, the verse that most of us learned first of all, Psalm 23:1, "The LORD is my shepherd; I shall not want." It sounds beautiful even when we merely read it, but how sweet it becomes when we stop and ponder it, weigh the meaning of the words, chew each word in it. When we ask ourselves first of all, "Who is my shepherd?" And then stop for a while to meditate upon the fact that it is JEHOVAH who is our Shepherd. Then ask ourselves, "*What* is Jehovah?" "My *Shepherd*." And then stop and think what is involved in being a shepherd and what it means to have Jehovah as our SHEPHERD. Then ask ourselves "Whose shepherd is Jehovah—*my* Shepherd." Not merely the Shepherd of men in general but *my own* Shepherd. A stranger entered a Presbyterian Church one day and was shown to a pew. The congregation rose to read the 23rd Psalm. A young lady sitting next to him, handed him one corner of her Bible as they read. As they read the first verse, he took a pencil out of his pocket and drew a line under the word "*my.*" When the service was over, the young lady said to him, "Do you mind telling me why you drew the line under the word 'my'?" "Well," he replied, "The Lord is my Shepherd. I was wondering if He were yours." Next dwell on the word, "*I,*" then on the word "*shall*" with all the certainty that there is in the word—then on the word, "*not,*" then on the word "*want*" and ask yourself all that is implied in the statement, "*I shall not want.*" Ah, the old familiar verse becomes so much sweeter as we eat it, chew and chew it and swallow it and digest it and assimilate it. If we thus eat different portions of the Bible day by day we would soon find a joy in it that we find in no other book. The only word that would express our relation to the Book would be "DELIGHT." The second of the two things that we must do is "*meditate in the law of the Lord day and night.*" These words tell us how to study the Word and when to study it.

(1) First, How to study it. "MEDITATE" therein. We live in a day in which meditation is largely a lost art. It is largely a lost art in all our study. We send our children to school; they are not allowed to think; they are simply crammed and crammed—we cram them with physiology, biology, psychology and all the rest of the ologies; until they themselves become mere *ape*-ologies for real thinkers. We try to see how many branches we can cover in a few years and how much of each branch we can cram in. A child in the grammar school grade has twelve studies; a child of thirteen will be set to writing a criticism on Tennyson's "In Memoriam." This is a good way to develop conceited fools, but it is no way to develop thinkers. Set a child of thirteen to criticizing Tennyson's "In Memoriam" and by the time she is eighteen she will be criticizing the Word of God itself. But cram, cram, cram, is the word of the hour in modern education. If our children studied fewer subjects and really studied and mastered those they did study, they would know more and be of more use in the world. But it is in Bible study especially that meditation is a lost art. We try to see how many chapters we can study in a single day. We get up a chart that covers the whole plan of the ages and all of God's dealing with men, angels and devils, from the eternity back of us to the eternity before us and expect to master it in thirty minutes or an hour. This is an excellent plan for making ourselves think that we are very wise— it is a miserable plan for getting the real nourishment out of the Word and the real "honey out of the rock." We should not so much say, "I will read so many chapters in a day," as "I will spend so much time each day in really studying and feeding upon the Book." Sometimes we will give to a single verse, or a single word, that will arrest our attention, all the time we put into Bible study that day. There is no greater enemy to successful study than hurry, and this is especially true of Bible study. One night I was teaching a Bible class in Minneapolis. A traveling man from New York, a very active member of St. George's Episcopal Church, dropped into my class. He had to take the train for the Far West soon after the class and I walked down to the station with him. As we walked he said to me, "Tell me in a word how to study my Bible." That is a pretty large contract to put *into a single word*, How to study the Bible, and I replied, "If I must put it into one word, that one word would be *Thoughtfully*. Think on what you study; look right at it, weigh it, weigh every word, turn it over and over and

over—meditate upon it."

But the words of the Psalmist tell us not merely how to study the Word but when to study it, "DAY AND NIGHT." Many people are asking, "Must I study the Bible fifteen minutes every day, or a half hour a day or two hours a day?" "Day and night," replies the Psalmist. This, of course, does not mean that we should be sitting with an open Bible before us every moment of the day and night. But it does mean that having had some regular time for Bible study, that after that time for Bible study is over we should carry away in our mind and heart what we have studied and meditate upon it as we go about our business, our household duties, or whatsoever we have to do. Oh, how much lighter and more pleasant the drudgery of life becomes if we go about it with the Word of God in mind and heart, meditating thereon in the midst of our wearing toil. I know of nothing else that will keep one in such perfect peace and abounding joy in these days of war and gloom and agony as meditating on the Word of God day and night.

III. The Result

And now what will be the result of our separating from the world in our walk, in our standing, in our sitting and of our delighting in the law of the Lord and meditating thereon day and night?

1. First of all, we will have *blessedness in heart.* "*Blessed* is the man," says our text that "walketh not," and so forth. The Hebrew word translated "blessed" is a very peculiar word in the Hebrew. It is not a participle at all, but a noun and a noun in the plural. Literally translated it would be "blessednesses of the man," that is, how manifold and varied is the blessedness and happiness of the man that does not do these three things and does do these two things. This world knows no joy so varied, so full, so manifold, so *wonderful* as the joy that comes to the one who is separated from the world and who meditates on the Word. I know all about the joy that comes from reading good literature; I have been a passionate devourer of books from early childhood. When I was a boy, I would get a book and hide away in some corner and devour it until my mother would come and say, "Oh, Archie, why don't you take your gun and go out hunting?" But all the joy that I have found in the study of the best literature, in the study of science, in the study of philosophy, can never for a moment com-

pare to the joy that I have found in meditating on the Word of God. So sweet has that joy become that oftentimes I am tempted to say that I will read no book but the Bible. I remember one night the first winter I was in Chicago. I had been very busy that day, answering my correspondence, and teaching in the Bible Institute in the morning, studying in the afternoon, and preaching that night. I got to my house late, after 11 o'clock, pretty thoroughly tired. I sat down for a little while to find rest in Bible study before I went to bed. I was reading the Bible through in course and had reached the last book in the Bible. In those days I did not care as much for that book as for other books—sometimes I had even been tempted to wish that the book was not in the Bible, but as that was where I was in my reading the Bible in course, I began reading the 11th chapter of the book. When I reached the 15th verse, "The kingdoms of this world shall become the kingdoms of our Lord and of His Christ, and he shall reign forever and ever," such joy swept into my soul as I took in the meaning of the words that I—do you know what I did? Of course you do. I shouted aloud. I was not brought up to shout in meeting. I was brought up in the Presbyterian and Episcopal churches. I never heard anyone say "Amen" except where it came in the regular place in the service until after I was in the ministry, and the first time a man said "Amen" when I was preaching it so upset me that I nearly lost the thread of my discourse. I cannot shout to this day in public, but, oh, when alone with God and His Book sometimes such a joy sweeps into the soul that nothing but a shout will give relief.

2. Second, we shall have *beauty of character*, "He shall be like a tree planted by the rivers of water." What is more beautiful than a well-watered tree in full leaf, the maples and the oaks and the beeches in the East, our palms and pepper trees and umbrella trees here in the West? Well, the one who refrains from doing the three things mentioned above and does the two things mentioned will be just like that tree in full leaf. His character will be full of beauty. If we had time, I could show you from the Word of God how every grace of character is the result of Bible study. The Psalmist says in Psalm 119:9, "Wherewithal shall a young man cleanse his way? by taking heed thereto according to thy word." In the 11th verse he says, "Thy word have I hid in my heart, that I might not sin against thee." Nothing else has the power to keep a man from sinning, and nothing else has the power to

adorn a man with all possible graces of character that the study of the Word of God has.

3. Third, we shall have *fruitfulness in service*. "Bringeth forth his fruit in his season." Do we not all long to be fruitful Christians? So many of us are fruitless. The great secret of being fruitful is intelligent study of the Word of God. The apostle Paul in writing to Timothy in 2 Timothy 3:16 says, "All Scripture is given by inspiration of God, and is profitable for doctrine, for reproof, for correction, for instruction in righteousness. That the man of God may be perfect, *thoroughly furnished unto all good works*." The Revised Version says, "complete, furnished completely unto every good work." How? Through what the apostle has just said, through the study of the inspired Word of God. A man may study everything else in the world, psychology, philosophy, pedagogy, and even theology, but if he does not study the Word of God, he is not fitted for real work for God. He will have no measure of success in winning souls. But a man may be quite ignorant of other branches of knowledge, but if he really studies and understands his Bible, he will have all the knowledge one needs to be a fruitful Christian and an efficient winner of souls.

4. Fourth, there will be one other result of not doing the three things and doing the two things, and that is *prosperity in everything*: "whatsoever he doeth shall prosper." Are we not all seeking for prosperity? There is no other way to get it than the way laid down in our text, but this road to prosperity is safe and sure. No one ever walked it without becoming prosperous in whatsoever he did. This, of course, does not mean necessarily that he will have what the world calls prosperity. He may not become a rich man, but he will have real prosperity in everything he undertakes. Some years ago I preached in Chicago a sermon on "The Power of the Word of God," or "The Advantages of Bible Study." I had in my congregation that morning a young man who was leading a rather defeated life. He was a Christian, but not a very effective Christian. He was a married man with a small family of children and was getting $12.50 a week. His work required him to get up at two or three o'clock in the morning to go on the market to buy for the house for which he worked. As he listened to the sermon that morning he made up his mind that instead of getting up at two o'clock or three o'clock in the morning, he would get up at one or two o'clock in the morning in order that he

might have a solid hour for Bible study before going to his work. He came on in his Christian experience by leaps and bounds and he came on in his business relations too. Within a year he went into business for himself. The first year he made $5,000 in his business, the next year I have been told that he made $10,000, and someone has told me that the next year he made $15,000, and he has gone on advancing from that day until this; but that is not the best of it, he came on in his Christian character and in his efficiency in Christian service. He is today one of the most used laymen in Chicago, identified with and a leader in every aggressive movement that is taken up by the Christians of the city, a tower of strength in his own church, a generous giver to the work of Christ at home and abroad, with three sons and one daughter following in his steps. "Whatsoever he doeth prospers."

Now I am not saying that if anyone will begin to study the Bible an hour a day he will spring from $12.50 a week to $5,000 a year, but I am saying, and what is better, God's Word says it, he will have real prosperity in everything he undertakes. Do you want blessedness in your heart, beauty in your character, fruitfulness in your service, and prosperity in everything you do—then stop walking in the counsel of the ungodly, stop standing in the way of sinners, stop sitting in the seat of the scornful and begin to delight in the law of the Lord and meditate therein day and night.

Study Questions

1. According to Psalm 1, what are three things we should not do?
2. On the contrary, what should we do?
3. What does it mean to eat the Word of God?
4. What will be the result of our meditation of the Word of God?

16

Love Contrasted,
Described, Exalted

1 Corinthians 13

Our subject this morning is Love Contrasted, Love Described, Love Exalted. Our text is the Corinthians. This chapter, which we are to study this morning is not only one of the most familiar, but also one of the most important and remarkable in the whole Bible. If there were no other proof of Paul's inspiration, this chapter would go far toward establishing it. The translation of the chapter found in the Revised Version is far better than that found in the King James Version, but by far the best translation of all is the translation into life. Every Christian should read and reread this chapter until mind and heart and will are saturated with it, until its fragrance distills itself in our every act and word and thought. The chapter naturally divides itself into three parts; the first part, verses 1–3, Love Contrasted, or the Absolute Indispensability of Love; the second part, verses 4–7, Love Described, or the Everyday Manifestations of Love; the third part, verses 8–13, Love Exalted, or the Peerless Preeminence of Love.

I. Love Contrasted or the Absolute Indispensability of Love

Let us first look at Love Contrasted, or the Indispensability of Love. "If I speak with the tongues of men and of angels, but have not love, I am become sounding brass, or a clanging cymbal. And if I have the gift of prophecy, and know all mysteries and all knowledge; and if I

151

have all faith so as to remove mountains but have not love, I am noth-ing." Here love is contrasted with five things in succession, each of which was held in great esteem in Corinth, and each of which is held in great esteem today. But Paul says no one of them, nor all of them together, will supply the lack of love.

1. *The first thing that Paul contrasts with love is the gift of tongues, and the gift of tongues in its highest conceivable form:* "Though I speak with the tongues of men and of angels." How the world would admire and applaud a man who could do that. A man upon whom the Spirit fell in such mighty power that not only the Pentecostal wonder would be repeated and Parthians and Medes and Elamites and Libyans and Ro-mans and Cretes and Arabians hear men talking in their own tongues, but also the man would talk with the tongue of angels as well as the tongues of men. That would be great and marvelous in the eyes of the world, but Paul says that even though that should happen, if that man had not love he would after all be only sounding brass or a clanging cymbal, just a brazen noise. The world looks at the eloquence on a man's lips. God looks at the love in his heart. Spiritual gifts are greatly to be desired; but the graces of the Spirit are far more to be de-sired, especially the grace of love (1 Cor. 12:31). We look oftentimes in wonder and admiration at the eloquent preacher, but God looks down into his heart and sees no love there, and says, "nothing but noise—sounding brass and a clanging cymbal."

2. *The second thing Paul contrasts with love is the gift of prophecy.* He describes this gift in the very highest form of its manifestation, "If I have the gift of prophecy, and know all mysteries and all knowledge." Surely this is something to be much coveted and greatly admired. Surely this will win God's applause. The man of great theological learn-ing and perfect spiritual vision must occupy a very high place in God's estimation. Listen to what God says, "even if a man have all this and have not love, he is NOTHING." Think of it, just nothing. How the world applauds the seer irrespective of what he is in heart, but God asks, "Is he also a lover?" If not, he is nothing, absolutely nothing.

3. *Now Paul brings forward a third thing and contrasts it with love—faith, miracle-working faith, miracle-working faith in the highest conceivable form, faith so as to remove mountains.* Surely this will count for some-thing with God. Surely this will give a man eminence in His sight. Even though a man is very faulty in character, if he can do wonders by

the power of faith, he must stand high not only in the estimation of man but God. Listen to what God says, "If I have all faith, so as to remove mountains, *but have not love* I am—NOTHING." Think of that—nothing! There are those in these days who are counting upon their gifts of healing and their extraordinary manifestations of faith to commend them to God. They would better ask themselves, "Have I love?" Some of them do not seem to have according to the description given in verses 4–7.

4. *Paul next brings forward a fourth thing that men count much on as commending them to God—magnificent giving,* "If I bestow all my goods to feed the poor." Surely a man who does that is a great man in God's sight. Surely he will get a rich reward. But the inspired apostle shakes his head, "not necessarily," he says, "you can give all you have, every dollar, every cent, and that too for the most philanthropic purpose, to feed the poor; but if you have not love, you will gain by it just *nothing.* How many false hopes that annihilates. Men with hearts full of selfishness are building great hopes for time and eternity upon the fact that they have given so much to the poor and to various charitable enterprises. But God puts the very searching question to you, "Have you love?" If not, your gifts will do you no more good than squandering your goods in riot and folly would. It will all profit you *nothing.*

5. *And now Paul takes up a fifth thing, and that which above all others is supposed to entitle one to a crown—martyrdom,* "If I give my body to be burned." Surely we have at last found one for whom God will have words of unstinting commendation—the brave martyr who marches to the stake for convictions, for truth, for right. For him there must be a sure and great reward, the martyr's crown. Listen, "and if I give my body to burned, *but have not love it profiteth me*—NOTHING." Oh, you who think so much and talk so much of what you have suffered for Christ, think of that. It all counts for nothing if you have not love.

There is nothing then, absolutely nothing, that will take the place of love. Gifts of speech, great knowledge of the deep things of God, miracle working faith, the greatest possible giving, extreme martyrdom, will not take the place of love. Nay, further, they count for nothing if love is lacking. One question then is driven home with tremendous emphasis to each one of our hearts, "Have you love?" This brings us to the second division of the chapter.

II. Love Described or the Everyday Manifestations of Love

God will not leave us in any self-deception or any doubt as to whether we have love or not. He gives a very plain description by which love can be known, wherever it exists, and by which its absence can be known wherever love is lacking. *Love has fifteen marks, not one of which is ever wanting where love exists.* We cannot dwell at great length upon each one, nor do we need to.

1. *The first mark of love is that it "suffereth long."* Love endures injury after injury, insult after insult, wrong after wrong, slander after slander, and still keeps right on loving and forgiving and forgetting. It wastes itself in vainly trying to help the unworthy and ungrateful, and still it loves on. That is the first mark of love. Do you show it?

2. *The second mark of love is, it "is kind."* It knows no harshness. It may be severe even as Jesus Himself was on occasion, but its necessary severity is shot through with gentleness and tenderness and pity. That is love.

3. *The third mark of love, "love envieth not."* Love knows no envy. How could it? He that really loves is as much interested in the welfare of others as in his own. How then can he envy? Does a mother ever envy the prosperity of her child? Is it not her chief delight? Love never envies, never. Do you love? Do you ever secretly grieve over and try to discount another's progress, temporal or spiritual? Then you have not love. You may speak with the tongues of men and of angels, you may have the gift of prophecy, know all knowledge, you have all faith so that mountains are disappearing before your onward march, you may be giving all your goods to feed the poor, you may be ready to die at the stake for your convictions, but you have not love, and you are nothing. Oh, friends, how often when we hear of another's prosperity or the great work of another Christian or church, how often we say, "Yes, but—ah—er." Or if we do not say it, we think it, and try to make the progress of the person or church not so much greater than our own after all. Why is this? Because we envy. And why do we envy? Because we have not love, and not having love we are nothing in God's sight.

4. *The fourth mark of love is that it "vaunteth not itself."* There is no surer mark of the absence of love and the dominance of selfishness

than that we talk about ourselves and our achievements. If we really love, the achievements of others will be more important to us than our own, and it is about them we will talk, "for out of the abundance of the heart the mouth speaketh" (Matt. 12:34).

5. *The fifth mark of love is that it is "not puffed up."* It is quite possible for one to have good sense enough not to vaunt himself, and yet in his heart be puffed up over his own virtues or victories. But love is not even puffed up. Love is so much taken up with the excellencies of others that it will not even dream of being inflated over its own.

6. *The sixth mark of love is that it "doth not behave itself unseemingly," that is, doth not do rude, ill-mannered, boorish things.* Love is considerate of the feelings of others and therefore avoids all that might offend or shock them. Nothing else will teach good manners and true etiquette as love will. Those professed Christians who delight in trampling all conventionalities underfoot and playing the boor are utterly lacking in one essential thing, love.

7. *"Love seeketh not its own."* These words need little comment. They demand exemplification rather than elucidation. It does, however, suggest a question. The question is a personal one: Are you seeking your own, or others' good? You haven't time to think it out now, but I hope you will get your Bible and think it out when you get home.

8. *"Love is not provoked."* The translators of the King James Version seem to have staggered at this statement, and so inserted a qualifying word, "love is not *easily* provoked." But that is not what God said. "Love is not provoked" was the statement. Love knows no irritation. It is often grieved, deeply grieved, but never irritated. How searching these words are! We get so hot over the unkind words that are spoken to us. I think some of us, as we read these words, will ask, "Have I any love? Am I not sounding brass or a clanging cymbal?"

9. *"Love taketh no account of evil."* Love never puts the wrong done it down in its books or in its memory. Some of us do. someone does us an injustice or a wrong of some kind, and we store it away in mind, and whenever we think of that person we think of the wrong they did us. That is not love. Love takes those pages of memory on which the wrongs done us are written and tears them up. If wrong is done it, it keeps no account of it.

10. Love *"rejoiceth not in unrighteousness."* It is not forever telling and glorying in the wrong that exists in individuals and church and

state. Brethren, why is it that some of us are so fond of dwelling on the evil that exists in church and state? I will tell you, we do not love.

11. *Love "rejoiceth with the truth."* Oh, if we love how our hearts will bound when we discover truth in others. How gladly we will call attention to it. This is a sure mark of love. Let me ask a question, Are you much given to that sort of thing? Some of you come and tell me this wrong and that wrong that you see in others. Don't you think it would be well to come occasionally and tell me of this excellence or that that you have discovered in others? Paul says that is the way love behaves.

12. *"Love beareth all things."* The word translated "beareth" means primarily "covereth" and may mean so here, though the New Testament usage is against it. That, however, will be quite true, love is always covering evil up. We are told in 1 Peter 4:8 that "love covereth a multitude of sins." The word translated covereth in this case is an entirely different one, however, from the one used in the passage before us. Love does not go around telling all the sin it has discovered in men; it hides it. That is a manifestation of love greatly needed in our day. But the words before us seem to mean more than that. They seem to mean that no matter what evil is done love, love bears it without revenge or complaint or bitterness or resentment.

13. *"Love believeth all things."* How proud some of us are of our powers to see through men and of the impossibility of getting the best of us. But that is not love, that is selfish shrewdness. Love is far greater than shrewdness. Love is very easily taken in. Indeed love would rather be deceived a hundred times than to misjudge once. "Love believeth all things," and when love has been deceived once it goes right on believing next time. We have heard it said of some men that they were forever being taken in by designing persons. Well, that speaks well for them, for "love believeth all things."

14. *"Love hopeth all things."* When it gets beyond believing, when one has proved a deceiver so often and is so manifestly a deceiver still that believing is simply impossible, then love hopes for the future. Love does not look at the bad as they now are, but as they may become by the transforming grace of God. When love looks at a drunkard, it does not see that poor, bloated, vile, enslaved thing that now is. It sees the clean, upright, intelligent, Christ-like man of God that is to be. When love looks at the troublesome sunday school scholar, it does not

see the shameless, vicious, unreasonable, almost idiotic boy that now is, but the attentive, obedient, gentlemanly boy that is to be. I tell you, friends, love is a great thing, but I fear it is a rare commodity.

15. Now comes the fifteenth and last mark of all, *"Love endureth all things."* When believing is impossible, when even hoping seems utterly out of the question, love endures. It does not get angry, it does not give up, it loves on, works on, endures on. Let Jesus serve as an illustration. How long Jesus has borne with men, but for love He has gotten back only reproach and sneers and spitting and blows and crucifixion. Reproach has broken His heart, and He is fast dying, but He summons all His waning strength, and cries, "Father forgive them, for they know not what they do" (Luke 23:24). That was love.

Friends, let me ask you a question again. Examined in the light of the fifteen marks of love Paul gives, have you much love? Have you any? If not, whatever else you may have, you are nothing.

III. Love Exalted, or the Peerless Preeminence of Love

We have no time left for the third division of the chapter, Love Exalted, or the Peerless Preeminence of Love. To sum it all up in a few words, prophecies, tongues, knowledge, have their day, love is eternal. God is love, and love partakes of His eternal nature. *"Love never faileth."* If you want something that will last, get love. All other things are partial, love is complete, perfect. There are three abiding things, faith, hope and love, but even of these three, the greatest is love.

Study Questions

1. Write out 1 Corinthians 13 in the translation of your choice.
2. What does Paul contrast love with?
3. What are the fifteen marks of love?

17

A Christ-like Man

There is one man who is pictured to us in the Bible who appears to be more like Christ than any other man of whose life we have an account. That man is Stephen, the first deacon in the Christian church, and the first Christian martyr. There is no fairer life recorded in history than that of Stephen, excepting, of course, the life of Him of whom Stephen learned and after whom he patterned. The character of Stephen presents a rare combination of strength and beauty, robustness and grace. Stephen occupies small space in the Bible, two chapters, Acts 6 and 7, and two verses in other chapters, Acts 11:19 and 22:20, yet in this short space a remarkably complete analysis of his character and the outcome of it is given.

I. Stephen's Character

Let us look first at Stephen's character. One word occurs again and again in the description of Stephen. It is the word *"full."* He was a remarkably full man.

1. First of all he was *"full of faith."* The record reads, "They chose Stephen, a man full of faith" (Acts 6:5). Stephen had unbounded confidence in God and in His Word; he believed implicitly in the certainty of every statement in the Word of God regarding the past, and he believed implicitly in its promises regarding the future. He had no fear of consequences when God's Word, or God's Spirit bade him do anything; he simply did it and left the consequences with God. It was God's to promise and to command; it was his simply to believe and obey what God said, and leave the outcome with God. Even in that awful moment when he was surrounded by a howling mob with

159

gnashing teeth, when the pitiless rocks were crushing his body and face and brain, he quietly looked up and said, "Lord Jesus, receive my spirit," and then kneeling down uttered a mighty prayer for his enemies, and gently "fell asleep." Oh, that we had more men and women of Stephen's faith, men and women who believe all God says and do all He commands in His Word and leave the results entirely with Him; men and women who walk straight on with childlike, unwavering confidence in Him in the path He marks out. There was never a day when men and women of that sort were more needed than today. Our power and our accomplishment will be proportionate to our faith in God and in His Word. Faith is the outstretched hand that helps itself to all God's fullness. The Lord Jesus is ever saying, *"According to your faith* be it unto you" (Matt. 9:29), and of many of us it must be said that Jesus "could do no mighty work there because of their unbelief" (Mark 6:5; Matt. 13:58).

2. In the next place Stephen was *"full of grace."* This we find in verse 8, Revised Version. The King James Version reads that he was "full of *faith* and power," but the Revised Version reads that he was "full of *grace* and power." It is true, as already seen, that he was full of faith, but he was full of something besides faith—"full of *grace.*" His faith in God and His Word brought the grace of God into his heart and life. He not only had grace, he was full of it—*"full* of grace." He was completely emptied of self, of his own will, of his own plans, of his own goodness, of his own thoughts, of his own strength, and the grace of God had just come in and taken complete possession of his heart and affections and will and character and life. This was the reason why he was so much like Christ Himself, Christ was just living His own life over again in Stephen. As we look at Stephen with his face shining like an angel's (Acts 6:15), and listen to the words that fall from his lips, it seems as if Jesus Himself had come back to earth again, and so He had: He had come back into Stephen's heart and was manifesting Himself in Stephen's life. And in the same way Jesus Christ is ready to come back again in your life and mine if we are only willing to be emptied of the self-life and filled with grace. Then we can say with the apostle Paul, "I have been crucified with Christ; and it is no longer I that live, but Christ liveth in me: and the life which I now live in the flesh I live in faith, the faith which is in the Son of God, who loved me, and gave Himself for me" (Gal.

2:20, RV). Ah! friends, most of us have some grace, but let us be full of grace, let us allow grace to fill every corner of our lives.

3. Stephen was also *"full of power!"* Grace and power are not one and the same thing, though all real power comes from grace, that is, it is a gift of God's grace. However, the graces of the Spirit are different from the gifts of the Spirit. "Love, joy, peace, longsuffering, gentleness, goodness, faith, meekness, and self-control" are the *graces* of the Spirit (Gal. 5:22). The various gifts of power for service are the *gifts* of the Spirit. Many a man has the graces of the Spirit in rich measure who has not much of the power of the Spirit in his work. Others have very much of the power of the Spirit in some directions, but are greatly lacking in the graces of the Spirit, but Stephen was full of faith, grace, and power, and so ought we to be. The graces of the Spirit ought to be richly revealed in our lives; the power of the Spirit ought to be mightily manifested in our work. It is the privilege of every believer to be a man of power in service. Grace and power are both at our disposal, grace for living like Christ, power for working like Christ (John 14:12). The men and women needed today are the men and women who live graciously and work mightily.

4. Stephen was also *full of the Word of God.* There is but one sermon of Stephen's recorded. You will find it in the seventh chapter of Acts. But what a sermon that one sermon is. It is Bible from beginning to end. When Stephen opened his mouth to speak the Scripture just flowed forth. As it is "out of the abundance of the heart that the mouth speaketh" (Matt. 12:34), it is evident that Stephen's heart was full of God's Word. He had pondered the Word of God deeply; he had discovered the deeper meanings of its precepts, promises, history, and prophecies; he had hidden the Word of God in his heart; he was full of the Word. This goes far toward explaining why he was also full of faith and grace and power. It is vain for one to pray to be full of faith if he neglects the Word of God, for "faith cometh by hearing, and hearing by the Word of God" (Rom. 10:17). I remember a time when I longed for faith, and tried hard to get it, but I never succeeded until I began feeding upon the Word of God. It is vain to seek for grace in the life and neglect the Word of God, for the Bible is "the Word of His grace, which is able to build you up" (Acts 20:32). It is vain to pray for power and neglect the Word of God, for it is when "the Word of God abideth in you" that "ye are *strong* and *overcome* the

wicked one" (1 John 2:14). Faith and grace and power all come from the Word of God, and in order to be full of them we must be full of it. How much we need today men and women like Stephen who are full of the Word of God, who have such a command of the Bible that none are "able to resist the wisdom by which" they speak, and men also who have the Word of God not only upon their lips, but in their hearts and lives. But we cannot be full of the Word of God if we do not study it, study it long and earnestly and prayerfully, study it (really study it) every day of our lives.

5. But Stephen was full of something else yet, he was *"full of the Holy Ghost"* (Acts 6:5). Being full of the Word of God and being full of the Holy Ghost go hand in hand. In Ephesians 5:18, 19, Revised Version, Paul says, "Be *filled with the Spirit;* speaking one to another in psalms and hymns and spiritual songs, singing and making melody in your heart to the Lord." And in Colossians 3:16 he says, "Let the *Word of Christ dwell in you richly* in all wisdom; teaching and admonishing one another in psalms and hymns and spiritual songs, singing with grace in your hearts to the Lord." By the comparison of these two passages we see that what in one place is attributed to being full of the Spirit, is in the other place attributed to being full of the Word of God. The two go naturally together, but they are often divorced. I know men who are full of the Word, that is, they have a very large technical and formal knowledge of the Word, but who are not full of the Spirit. They are well instructed but they have no unction. They are dry as chips. Indeed, I have known men who were once full of the Spirit, but they have lost the manifestation of His presence and of His power. As far as the form of knowledge of the Word goes, they know as much as they ever did, but the power has gone out of their words. But Stephen was "full of the Spirit" of God as well as full of the Word of God. His enemies were not able to resist, not only "the wisdom," but also *the Spirit* by which he spake" (Acts 6:10). Let us seek to be full of the Holy Ghost. Without this our lives will be graceless and our efforts will be powerless. The Holy Spirit's power was manifested in Stephen, as we have already seen, in a twofold way: in his life, and in his work.

6. Stephen was also *full of love*. In Acts 7:57–60 we see how absolutely his whole inner and outer life were under the control of love. In no other man, perhaps, except Christ, has love shone out as it did

in Stephen. Look at Stephen as he falls beneath the stones hurled at him by his infuriated antagonists and assassins. He can no longer stand, and he sinks to his knees. His crushed forehead is throbbing with pain, his strength is fast waning, but he summons all his remaining strength and utters a loud cry. What is it? Is it, "Lord curse these my murderers"? No, "Lord, lay not this sin to their charge." Here we see love for enemies triumphant even in death. There is perhaps no lesson of Stephen's life harder to learn than this, and yet there is no other lesson that we more need to learn than this, and there was never a time when we more needed to learn it than today, when we are face to face with a mighty foe who may do us or our loved ones awful harm. Let us never forget to be full of love. Love is the one divine thing. "If I speak with the tongues of men and of angels, but have not love, I am become sounding brass, or a clanging cymbal" (1 Cor 13:1, RV). Ah! it is easy to love the lovely, in fact it is not hard to have a certain sentimental love for the unlovely, provided they have never crossed our path in any way; but to love the one who lies about you, as these did about Stephen, this is the hard thing, this is the supreme test of whether the Lord Jesus be indeed dwelling in us or not. There are many of us here today who have coveted earnestly that we might be full of faith and grace, and power, and the Word of God, and the Holy Spirit, but are you full of love? Do you really wish to be full of love? Remember in answering that question that while love is the divinest thing in the world, it is also the most costly.

7. Stephen was not only full of love, he was also *full of courage*. Many men seem to be forgiving simply because they have not sufficient energy of character to be vengeful, but Stephen's forgiveness was not of that kind. He was a man of almost matchless energy and fearless courage; he knew the Jews, he knew what they had done to his Lord, and yet, knowing their history, he faces his angry antagonists and boldly says: "Ye stiffnecked and uncircumcised in heart and ears, ye do always resist the Holy Ghost; as your fathers did, so do ye. Which of the prophets have not your fathers persecuted? and they have slain them which shewed before of the coming of the Just One" (Acts 7:51, 52), and then when they gnashed upon him with their teeth, he beat no retreat; but looking up steadfastly into heaven, and seeing the glory of God, and Jesus standing on the right hand of God, he says, "Behold, I see the heavens open, and the Son of man

standing on the right hand of God" (Acts 7:56). Do we not sorely need courage like that today, courage to face the enemies of Christ, and to give our uncompromising testimony for Him? How unlike this is to the timid, cringing, sentimentality and gush that passes for Christianity today. We need Stephens in business, we need Stephens in society, we need Stephens in public affairs, we need Stephens in the home and in the church.

There was then this seven-fold fullness in Stephen: he was "full of faith," "full of grace," "full of power," full of the Word of God, "full of the Holy Ghost," full of love, full of courage.

8. There was one more thing about Stephen's character that needs to be noted, he was *a man of prayer.* Prayer was the spontaneous utterance of his heart in the hour of trouble. The last two utterances of his life were prayers (Acts 7:59, 60) just as were two of the last utterances of his Master, and Stephen's prayers were closely modeled after those of his Master. No man can be a man of power who is not a man of prayer. No man can be full of grace who is not a man of prayer. No man can be full of the Holy Ghost who is not a man of prayer. Of all the sad neglects in present-day Christian living there is perhaps none so sad and fatal as the neglect of prayer. Why is there so much striving after holiness and so little obtaining of it? Neglect of prayer. Why is there so much machinery in the church and so little real work turned out? Neglect of prayer. Why is there so much preaching and so few conversions? Neglect of prayer. Why is there so much Christian enterprise and so little Christian progress? Neglect of prayer. What the church of Christ needs today above all else, as in the day of Jonathan Edwards, is a call to prayer. What the individual church and the individual Christian needs today is a call to prayer. Oh, that some mighty voice might be heard sounding from the Atlantic to the Pacific, and then around the world: LET US PRAY. Our nation today is at the greatest crisis in its history, and what our nation needs today above all else is prayer, real prayer, prayer by multitudes of men and women who know how to pray. The great majority of our statesmen are right when they say that the great need of our day is preparedness, but the preparedness that we need is not the preparedness that is wrought out by Germanizing our land, building up a vast military system; it is the preparedness that is wrought out by prayer.

II. The Outcome of Stephen's Character

There is little time left to dwell upon the outcome of Stephen's character and life.

1. *His face shone like an angel's* (Acts 6:15). The face of any man who is full of faith, and grace, and of the Spirit, and of the Word of God, and of power, and of love, will shine.

2. *He preached with unanswerable wisdom and resistless power* (Acts 6:10).

3. He *"wrought great wonders and signs"* (Acts 6:8).

4. *"The Word of God increased, and the number of the disciples multiplied in Jerusalem exceedingly"* (Acts 6:7). The Word of God is bound to increase, and the number of disciples is bound to multiply exceedingly when we have deacons and workers like Stephen.

5. Men were *"cut to the heart"* by his preaching (Acts 7:54). The preaching of such a man, full of the Holy Ghost, is sure to bring deep conviction. Our Lord told His disciples that when the Holy Ghost was come He would "convict the world in respect of sin." There will be convicting power in the preaching and personal work of any man or woman who is full of the Holy Ghost.

6. But this conviction in Stephen's case did not result in conversion. As men could not gainsay the truth of what he said, they took to lying about the preacher (Acts 6:13). But they did not stop at that, they gnashed upon him with their teeth (Acts 7:54), and they did not stop at that, they stoned and killed him (Acts 7:58–60). This is the sort of treatment that a man like Stephen may expect from a God-hating and Christ-hating, and truth-hating world. In all probability there will be conviction of sinners and conversion of sinners, but sooner or later there will be hatred and persecution and suffering, and maybe death.

7. But there was another outcome of Stephen's character, Stephen had his exceeding great reward, a reward that far more than compensated for the cruel treatment that he suffered. *The heavens were opened* and he saw Jesus and the glory of God (Acts 7:55), then he gently fell asleep and departed to be with Christ, which was "very far better" (Acts 7:59, 60; cf. Phil. 1:23), and out of that seemingly fruitless sermon and triumphant death there sprang the prince of apostles, Paul.

Paul and all his mighty ministry and all the results of that wonderful ministry were the outcome of what Stephen was.

Study Questions

1. What aspects of Stephen's character are visible in Scripture?
2. What was the outcome of Stephen's character?

18

Walking as Jesus Walked

He that saith he abideth in Him, ought himself also to walk even as He walked (1 John 2:6).

The one great secret of a life full of blessedness is abiding in Christ. Abiding in Christ is the one all-inclusive secret of power in prayer: our Lord Jesus says in John 15:7, "If ye abide in me, and my words abide in you, ask whatsoever ye will and it shall be done unto you." Abiding in Christ is also the secret of fruitfulness: our Lord Jesus says, "I am the vine, ye are the branches: he that abideth in me, and I in him, the same beareth much fruit: for apart from me ye can do nothing." And abiding in Christ is the secret of fullness of joy: in the same chapter to which we have referred twice, the Lord Jesus says, "These things have I spoken unto you [i.e., these things about abiding in Him], that my joy may be in you, and that your joy may be made full," a clear statement that our joy is made full, or filled full, when we abide in Him, and him alone. But according to our text this morning, the one proof that we do abide in Him is that we walk even as He walked. The great test of whether we are abiding in Christ or not is not some ecstatic feeling, but our daily conduct. If we walk as He walked that is proof, conclusive proof, that we are abiding in Him whether we have ecstatic feelings or not. On the other hand if we do not walk as He walked, that is conclusive proof that we are not abiding in Him, no matter how many ecstasies and raptures of which we may boast. So the practical question that faces each one of us this morning is, Am I walking as Jesus walked? This brings us face to face with the question, How did Jesus walk?

I. How Jesus Walked

Some years ago Charles Sheldon brought out a book named "In His Steps," in which he tried to imagine how Jesus would act in various imaginary relations of life; how, for example, He would conduct a newspaper, and so forth. The book awakened a great deal of interest, but was necessarily not very satisfactory. We are not left to our own imaginations in this matter. Far more practical than the question of what Jesus would do in various imaginary relations of life is to find what He actually did when He was here on earth, and find out how He really walked. How did Jesus walk?

1. First of all *He walked with an eye absolutely single to the glory of God.* He says in John 8:50, "I seek not mine own glory." In no act of His whole life did He have regard to His own honor or glory, He was entirely absorbed in the glory of Him that sent Him. In the prayer which He offered the night before His crucifixion He said, "Father, the hour is come: glorify thy Son." Now that looks at the first glance as if He were seeking His own glory, but listen to the rest of the petition: "that the Son may glorify Thee." It was not His own glory that He was seeking, but altogether the Father's, and He simply asked the Father to glorify Him that the Father Himself might be glorified. In the 4th verse of the same chapter we hear Him saying, "I glorified Thee on the earth, having accomplished the work which Thou gavest me to do." His own glory was a matter about which He was entirely unconcerned; the glory of the Father was the one thing that absorbed Him. In every act of His life, small or great, He was simply seeking the glory of God. He had an eye absolutely single to the glory of God. Even in the eternal world, before He became incarnate, when He was existing in the form of God, when the whole angelic world saw by His outward form that He was a divine person, and when He might have retained that divine glory, "He thought it not a thing to be grasped to be on an equality with God, but emptied Himself and took upon Him the form of a servant and was made in the likeness of men, and being found in fashion as a man He humbled Himself, becoming obedient even unto death, yea, the death of the cross" (Phil. 2:5–8) because by this giving up His own divine glory and taking upon Himself humility and shame, greater glory would come to the Father. And now may I put the question to you, and to myself as I put it to

you, are you walking with an eye absolutely single to the glory of God? Is there but one thing that concerns you in determining upon any course of action, namely, will I glorify the Father more by doing this than by not doing it? I heard two Christian women discussing the other day the relative merits of the East and West as a place to live. One spoke about the maples and the oaks and the beeches of the East, about the various social and other advantages. The other dwelt upon the fruits and flowers of Southern California, upon the air and the cleanliness. But if we are to walk as Jesus walked, we will not determine our home by such considerations as these, the whole question will be will it be more to God's glory for me to live in the East or the West?

2. In the second place, we find from a study of the walk of Jesus as recorded in the four Gospels, that *He walked in whole-hearted surrender to and delight in the will of the Father.* Not only could He say, "I do always the things that are pleasing to Him," but He even went so far as to say, "My meat," that is, His sustenance and delight, "is to do the will of Him that sent me, and to accomplish His work." The circumstances under which He said this were significant; He was tired, hungry, and thirsty, so tired that when His disciples went into the neighboring village to buy food for Him and them, He was unable to go along, but rested wearily upon the well at Sychar. As he rested there He looked up the road and saw a sinful woman coming toward Him. In His joy in an opportunity of doing the Father's will in winning that lost woman He entirely forgot His weariness and His hunger, and step by step led her to the place where she knew Him as Christ. At that moment His disciples again appeared and wondered that He was talking with a woman, and then urged Him to eat of the food which they had brought from the village, saying, "Rabbi, eat." He looked up at them almost in wonder and said, "I have meat to eat that ye know not." In other words, He says, "I am not hungry; I have been eating." The disciples were filled with surprise and said one to another, "Hath any man brought Him aught to eat?" Then Jesus answering their thoughts said, "My meat is to do the will of Him that sent me, and to accomplish His work." All the joy He asked, all the gratification He asked was an opportunity to do the Father's will. He not only did His Father's will always, but He delighted in doing it, it was His chief gratification, the very sustenance of His innermost being.

Are you walking as Jesus walked? Are you walking in whole-hearted surrender to the will of God, studying His Word daily to find out what that will is, doing it every time when you find it, finding your chief delight in doing the will of the Father, no matter how disagreeable in itself that will may be? This is the way Jesus walked. Are you walking as He walked?

3. Furthermore, *He walked in utter disregard of self.* This is involved in what we have already said, but we mention it separately in order to make it clear. His own interests, His own ease, His own comfort, His own honor, His own anything were nothing to Him. "Though He was rich, yet for our sakes He became poor, that we through His poverty might become rich" (2 Cor. 8:9). Not His own interests, but those of others were His sole consideration. What riches did He give up? The greatest that anyone ever knew; all the possessions and glory of God. How poor did He become? The poorest man the world ever saw. He not only became a man, taking all a man's dishonor upon himself, He became a poor man, a despised man. When He went out of this world He went out of it stripped of everything. He had not had food for many long hours; every shred of clothing was torn from Him as they nailed Him to the cross; He was stripped of all honor and re-spect, lifted up on the cross as a condemned felon, while jeering mobs passed by mocking Him, and this end He Himself chose because by thus emptying Himself of everything He secured eternal life and an inheritance incorruptible, undefiled and that passeth not away, for others. His own interests were nothing, the interests of others were everything. Are you walking as Jesus walked? Are you living your life day by day in utter disregard of your own interests, your own repu-tation, your own authority, your own comfort, your own honor, doing the things that will bring blessing to others, no matter what loss and dishonor the doing of them may bring to you? "He that saith he abideth in Him, ought himself also to walk even as He walked."

4. Furthermore, *He walked with a consuming passion for the salva-tion of the lost.* He Himself has defined the whole purpose of His com-ing into this world; in Luke 19:10 He says, "The Son of man came to seek and to save that which was lost." He had just one purpose in leav-ing heaven and all its glory and coming down to earth with all its shame, that was the seeking out and saving of the lost. The saving of the lost was the consuming passion of His life. For this He came, for

this He lived, for this He prayed, for this He worked, for this He suffered, for this He died. Are you walking with such a consuming passion for the salvation of the lost? Oh, how many are there of us who indeed are doing something for the salvation of the lost, but what we do is perfunctory; we do it simply because we think it is the thing we ought to do, not because there is a consuming passion within that will not let us rest without doing everything in our power to save the lost, to bring the lost to a saving knowledge of Jesus Christ. If the professedly Christian men and women walked with such a consuming passion for the salvation of the lost as Jesus walked, how long would it be before hundreds and thousands were turning to Christ here in Los Angeles.

5. *He walked in a life of constant prayerfulness.* In Hebrews 5:7 we read that in the days of His flesh He "offered up prayers and supplications with strong crying and tears." His whole life was a life of prayer. The record that we have of His life in the four Gospels is very brief, only eighty-nine very short chapters in all, and yet in this very brief account of the life of our Lord the words "pray" and "prayer" are used in connection with Him no less than twenty-five times, and His praying is mentioned in places where these words are not used. People wonder what Jesus would do in this relation or that, but the Bible tells us plainly what He actually did, He prayed. He spent much time in prayer. He would rise a great while before day and go out into the mountain to pray alone. He spent whole nights in prayer. If we are to walk as Jesus walked, we must lead a life of prayerfulness. The man who is not leading a life of prayer, no matter how many excellent things he may be doing, is not walking as Jesus walked.

6. *He also walked a walk characterized by a diligent study of the Word of God.* We see this in many things. His whole thought and the things that He said showed that He was saturated with Old Testament Scripture. He met each one of the three assaults of Satan in His temptation in the wilderness with a quotation from the Old Testament, and we read in Luke 24:27 that "beginning from Moses and from all the prophets, He interpreted to them in all the Scriptures," conclusively showing that He had pondered long and deep all parts of the Old Testament, the only written Word of God then existing, and in the 44th verse of the same chapter we read that He said, "All things must be

fulfilled which are written in the law of Moses, and the prophets, and the Psalms, concerning me." He himself was the incarnate Word of God, nevertheless, He diligently studied and steeped Himself in the written Word in so far as it then existed. Are you in this matter walking as Jesus walked? Are you digging into the Bible? Are you saturating yourself with the Word of God? Are you permitting your whole thought and the very language you use to be saturated with Scripture? It was thus that Jesus walked, with an eye absolutely single to the glory of God, in whole-hearted surrender to and delight in the will of the Father, in utter disregard of self, with a consuming passion for the salvation of the lost, with a life of constant prayerfulness, in diligent study of the Word of God. Are you thus walking? Many of us doubtless will have to say this morning, "I am not," and that brings us to the next question.

II. How Can We Walk as Jesus Walked?

It is a very practical question, and the all-sufficient answer to it is in our text: "He that saith he *abideth in Him*, ought himself also to walk even as He walked." It is clear from this that there is only one way by which we can walk as He walked, and that is by abiding in Him. But what does that mean? Our Lord Himself has explained this in John 15:1–5. In these verses He tells us that He is the vine and we are the branches, and that if we would bear fruit and power in prayer, and joy, we must abide in Him, just as the branch that bears fruit must abide in the vine. That is to say, abiding in Him is maintaining the same relation to Him that a fruitful branch of a grapevine bears to the vine; it has no life of its own, all its life is the inflow of the life of the vine, its buds and leaves and blossoms and fruit are not its own, but simply the outcome of the life of the vine flowing into it and bearing fruitage through it, so that if we are to abide in Him and bear fruit, we must seek to have no life of our own, we must renounce all our self-efforts after righteousness, not simply renounce our sins, but renounce our own thoughts, our own ambitions, our own purposes, our own strength, our own everything, and cast ourselves in utter dependence upon the Lord Jesus for Him to think His thoughts in us, to will His purpose in us, to choose His choice through us, to work out His own glorious perfection of character in us. Many try to be like Christ by imitating Christ. It is absolutely impossible for us to imitate Christ in our own strength. The most discouraging thing that any earnest-minded man can attempt is to imitate Christ. Nothing else will plunge a man in deeper despair than to try to imitate Christ in his own strength. Instead of imitating Him we should open our hearts wide for Him to come in and live His own life out through us. Christ in us is the secret of a Christian life. The only Christ that many professed Christians know is the historic Christ, that is the Christ who lived nineteen centuries ago on this earth and died on the cross of Calvary, an atoning sacrifice for sin. They only know the Christ who died for us on the cross. Oh, we need to know something further than that if we are to be like Him; we need to know a living Christ today, a Christ who not only arose and ascended to the right hand of the Father, but a Christ who has come down and dwells in us, the hope of glory (Col. 1:27). From the bottom of my heart I praise God for Christ for us on the cross. All my hope of acceptance before God is built upon Him bearing my sins in His own body on the cross, and I do praise God for Christ for us. But, oh, how I praise God, not only for Christ for me on the cross, but for Christ in me, a living, personal Christ in me today, living His life out through me, and causing me to walk even as Jesus walked. How we may thus have Christ in us Paul tells us in Galatians 2:20, American Revised Version. He says, "I have been crucified with Christ," that is, when Christ was crucified on the cross He was crucified as our representative and we were crucified in Him, and we must see ourselves where God put us on the cross in the place of death and the curse, and thus cease to live in our own strength. Then he goes on to say, "It is no longer I that live, but Christ liveth in me;" that is, as he had been crucified with Christ he counted himself what he really was in his standing before God, dead, and as a dead man, no longer sought to live his own life, but let Jesus Christ live His life out through him. And then he goes on still further to say, "That life which I now live in the flesh I live in faith, the faith which is in the Son of God, who loved me and gave Himself for me." The whole secret of being like Christ is found in these words. We must count self dead; we must give up our self-efforts after likeness to Christ; we must distrust our own strength as much as we distrust our own weakness and our own sin, and instead of striving to live like Christ, let Christ live in us, as He longs to do. Of course we cannot thus have Christ in us until we know Christ for us, making a full atonement for our sins on the cross. Paul explains the whole secret of it in another way in Ephesians 3:16–20. Here he prays for the believers in Ephesus that they "may be strengthened with power through His Spirit in the inner man; that Christ may dwell in your hearts through faith." The thought is, it is the work of the Holy Spirit to form an indwelling Christ within us, and the way to know Christ in us is to let the Holy Spirit form Him within us.

Are you walking as Jesus walked? Do you wish to walk as Jesus walked, cost whatever it may? Well then, realize that you have not been walking as Jesus walked, and that the reason you have not walked as Jesus walked is because you have been trying to do it yourself, and give up your own attempts to do it and just look up to the risen Christ, through whose death on the cross you have found pardon and justification, and let Him come and dwell in you and live His life out through you; to have His perfect will in you, and just trust the Holy Spirit to form this indwelling Christ in your heart.

Study Questions

1. How did Jesus walk?
2. How can we walk as Jesus walked?

19

The Secret of Abiding Peace, Abounding Joy, and Abundant Victory in War Times and at All Times

Enoch walked with God: and he was not; for God took him (Gen. 5:24).

Our subject this morning is The Secret of Abiding Peace, Abounding Joy, and Abundant Victory in War Times and at All Times. You will find the text in Genesis 5:24, "Enoch walked with God: and he was not; for God took him." In this description of Enoch's walk we find the secret of abiding peace, abounding joy, and abundant victory in war times and at all times. To my mind the text is one of the most fascinating and thrilling verses in the entire Bible. It sounds more like a song from a heavenly world than a plain statement of historical facts regarding a humble inhabitant of this world of ours, but such it is, and it is possible for each one of us to so live and act that it may be recorded of us, "He walked with God," and later, "and he was not; for God took him." The position of this verse in the Bible is significant and suggestive. There has been, in the verses immediately preceding, a very prosaic, monotonous, and at first sight tedious recital of how one man after another of the olden time lived so many years, begat a son, continued to live so many years and begat sons and daughters and then died. Then suddenly Enoch is introduced and the story begins just as the other stories begin and goes on just as the other stories go on, and seems about to end just as the other stories end, but no, there is this fresh breath from heaven and these melodious tones sound out: "And Enoch walked with God: and he was not; for God took him." Then the story goes on again in the same old strain. Remember that this account belongs to a far-away time, thousands of years before Christ, and about a thousand years before the flood, and yet what depth of truth and beauty there is in it. Are there not lessons for us to learn from that far, far away olden time? The entire authentic history of Enoch is contained in nine verses in the Bible, six in the Old Testament, three in the new. History outside of the Bible is utterly unacquainted with him, yet he stands out as one of the most remarkable and admirable men of whom history speaks, a man whom God honored as He has but one other member of the entire race. His greatness was of the kind that pleases God. We are told in the 11th chapter of Hebrews and the 5th verse that "he hath had witness borne to him that before his translation he had been well pleasing to God." Quite likely his greatness did not win very hearty commendation from his contemporaries. However, that was not of much consequence. His greatness did not consist of military renown, political power, profound scholarship, successful statesmanship, splendid artistic or architectural genius, nor even magnificent philanthropic achievement. It was greatness of a more quiet and less pretentious and visible nature, but of a far more real and lasting nature; it was greatness of character, *"he walked with God,"* and God so enjoyed his society that he took him to be with Himself permanently.

I wish to make clear to you all today three things: first, what it is to walk with God; second, what are some of the results of walking with God; third, how we may get into such a walk ourselves.

I. What Is It to Walk with God?

First of all then what is it to walk with God? I think I may safely say that with some of us here this morning that question needs no answer, God Himself has answered it to us in blessed, unspeakably blessed experience. But with some of us—yes, many of us—it does need an answer. We have read the words of the text before, perhaps we have read them often. They have charmed us, soothed us, thrilled us, and yet often the question has arisen in our hearts, just what do they mean. This question admits of a very plain and simple answer: to walk with God means to live one's life in the consciousness of God's presence and in conscious communion with Him, to have the thought constantly before us, "God is beside me," and to be every now and then speaking to Him, and still more listening for Him to speak to us. In a word, to walk with God is to live in the real, constant, conscious companionship of God. We read that Enoch walked with god, not on a few rare occasions of spiritual exaltation, such perhaps as most of us have known, but for three hundred consecutive years after the birth of Methuselah (Gen. 5:22). It is possible for us to have this consciousness of the nearness and fellowship of God in our daily life, to talk with Him as we talk to an earthly friend; yes, as we talk to no earthly friend, and to have Him talk to us, and to commune with Him in a silence that is far more meaningful than any words could be. I would gladly linger here in this sweet and holy place, but let us pass on to the results of walking with God.

II. The Results of Walking with God

1. The first result of walking with God is *great joy, abounding joy.* "In thy presence," sings the Psalmist, "is *fullness of joy*" (Ps. 16:11). There is no greater joy than that which comes from right companionship. Who would not rather live in a hut with congenial companions than in a palace with disagreeable associates? Who would not rather live on a bleak and barren isle among real Christians than in the fairest land the sun ever shone upon among infidels, blasphemers, drunkards, ruffians and libertines? The most attractive feature of heaven is its society, especially the society of God and the Lord Jesus. Well might Samuel Rutherford say: I would rather be in hell with Thee than in heaven without Thee: for if I were in hell with Thee that would be heaven to me, and if I were in heaven without Thee that would be hell to me." But when we have the conscious presence and companionship of God on earth, "we have two heavens, the heaven to which we are going and a heaven to go to heaven in." In one of the loneliest hours of His lonely life Jesus looked up with radiant joy and said, "Yet I am not alone, because the Father is with me" (John 6:32).

Can you not remember some ecstatic hour of your life when you walked, and sometimes talked and sometimes were silent, with an earthly companion whom you loved as you loved no other? Oh, happy hour! but only faintly suggestive of the rapture that comes from walking with God, for He is an infinitely dearer and better and more glorious companion than any earthly one could be. How the mundane details of everyday life are transfigured if we have the constant fellowship of God in them. There lived in the Middle Ages a lad named Nicholas Hermann. He was a raw, awkward youth, breaking all things that he touched, but one day the thought was brought to his mind with great force that God was everywhere and that he might have the constant thought of His presence with him and do all things to His glory. This thought transformed his life. He soon went to a monastery. His duty there was of the most menial character, in the kitchen, washing pots and kettles, but to use his own way of putting it, he "practiced the presence of God" in the midst of his humble toil. That kitchen became so holy a place that men took long journeys to meet Nicholas Hermann and to converse with him. Some of his conversations and letters have been published under the title "The Practice of the Presence of God."

2. The second result of walking with God is *a great sense of security, abiding peace*. In the Psalm already quoted the Psalmist sings again: "I have set the Lord always before me, because He is at my right hand I shall not be moved" (Ps. 16:7). Certainly not. How can we be moved if God is with us, what harm can befall us? How often God says to His servants as they begin to tremble before approaching danger: "Fear not, I am with thee" (Is. 41:10). How safe the trusting child feels with father or mother by its side. A little girl was once playing in a room below while her mother was above, busy about household duties. Every little while the child would come to the foot of the stairs and call up: "Mamma, are you there?" "Yes, darling, what is it?" "Nothing, I only wanted to know if you were there." Then again in a little while: "Mamma, are you there?" "Yes, darling, what is it?" "Nothing, I only wanted to know you were there." Ah! is not that all we want to know, that God is here, right here by our side? There may be pestilence, there may be war, there may be famine, there may be thugs upon the street, there may be burglars in the house, there may be haunts of sin, and unprincipled men and women on every hand; yes our wrestling may not be with flesh and blood but "against the principalities, against the powers, against the world rulers of this darkness, against the spiritual hosts of wickedness in the heavenlies," but what does it

matter? God is with us. Oh, if we only bore in mind at every moment the thought of His presence with us, if we could only hear Him saying, "Fear thou not, for I am with thee; be not dismayed, for I am thy God: I will strengthen thee; yea I will help thee; yea I will uphold thee with the right hand of my righteousness," there would never be one single tremor of fear in our hearts under any circumstances. No matter how the war increases, no matter how near it may come to our own doors, there would be unruffled calm, abounding peace, we could constantly say under all circumstances, "The Lord is my light and my salvation; whom shall I fear? The Lord is the strength of my life; of whom shall I be afraid? When the wicked, even my enemies and my foes came upon me to eat up my flesh, they stumbled and fell. Though a host should encamp against me, my heart shall not fear: though war should rise against me, in this will I be confident." No wonder the Psalmist wrote in this connection, *"One thing* have I desired of the LORD, that will I seek after; that I may dwell in the house of the LORD all the days of my life, to behold the beauty of the LORD, and to inquire in His temple." The conscious companionship of God is the great secret of abiding peace.

3. The third result of walking with God is *spiritual enlightenment.* Communion with God rather than scholarship opens to us the mind and thought of God. There is no hint that Enoch was a man of science or letters. I am very sure he was not a higher critic, and yet this plain man by walking with God and talking with God got such an insight into the purposes of God as no other man of his time had. In the epistle of Jude, the 14th and 15th verses, we learn that even in that far-away day, a thousand years before the flood, Enoch got hold of the great truth of the second coming of Christ. So today some old washerwoman, some humble cobbler, who walks with God may know more of the mind of God than many an eminent college professor, or even professor in a theological seminary. The important question concerning points in dispute in religion and spiritual life is not what do the scholars say, but what do the men and women who walk with God say. If one is considering going to someone for spiritual instruction, the first question is not how much of a scholar is he, not how much does he know of Latin and Hebrew and Greek and Syriac and philosophy and psychology, but does he walk with God. This is the great condition of spiritual insight, wisdom and understanding.

4. The fourth result of walking with God is *purity of heart and life*. Nothing else is so cleansing as the consciousness of God's presence. Things that we have long tolerated become intolerable when we bring them into the white light of the presence of the Holy One. How many things we do in the darkness of the night, yea, even in the broad light of day, that we could not for a moment think of doing if we realized God was right there by our side—*looking*. Many deeds we now do would be left undone if we realized this. Many words we now speak would be left unspoken, many thoughts and fancies we now cherish would be speedily banished. There are certain things that we do in the absence of certain holy friends that we would not for a moment do in their presence, but God is always present whether we know it or not, and if we walk in the consciousness of His presence, if we walk with God, our lives and hearts will speedily whiten. I have a friend who in his early life, though he professed to be a Christian, was very profane. He tried hard to overcome his profanity, but failed. He felt he must give up his attempt to be a Christian, but one day a wise Christian to whom he appealed for help, said to him, "Would you swear if your father were present?" "No." "Well, when you go to your work tomorrow remember that God is with you every moment. Keep the thought of God's presence with you." At the end of the day to his amazement he had not sworn once. He had had the thought of God with him through the day and he could not be profane in that presence. The consciousness of the presence of God will keep us from doing all the things that we would not dream of doing in His presence. Herein lies the secret of a holy life.

5. The next result of walking with God is closely akin to this, *beauty of character*. We become like those with whom we habitually associate. How like their parents children become. How many mothers and fathers have been startled by seeing their own imperfections and follies mirrored in their children. Husband and wife grow strangely like one another, thus also the one who associates with God becomes like God. John Welch, a spiritual hero of the 16th century (1590 A.D.), son-in-law of John Knox, is said to have "reckoned that day ill-spent if he stayed not seven or eight hours in prayer." One who well-remembered his ministry said of him: "He was a type of Christ." Association with God made him like God. If we walk with God, more and more will his beauty illumine and reflect itself in our lives. Moses'

very face shone as he came down from the forty days and forty nights of converse with God. So will our whole life soon shine with a heavenly glow and glory if we habitually walk with God. "With unveiled faces reflecting as a mirror the glory of God" we shall be "transformed into the same image from glory unto glory" (2 Cor. 3:18).

6. The next result of walking with God will be *eminent usefulness*. Our lives may be quiet and even obscure, it may be impossible to point to what men call great achievement, but the highest usefulness lies not in such things but in the silent, almost unnoticed but potent and pervasive influence of a holy life, whose light illumines, whose beauty cheers, and whose nobility elevates all who come in contact with it. Enoch has wrought out immeasurably more good for man than Nebuchadnezzer, who built the marvelous structures of Babylon, than Augustus who "found Rome brick and left it marble," than the Egyptian monarchs who built the pyramids to amaze and mystify the world for thousands of years to come; and today the man or woman, no matter how humble or obscure, who walks with God is accomplishing more for God and man than Morse with his telegraph, Fulton with his steamboat, Stevenson with his locomotive, Cyrus Field with his Atlantic cable, Roebling with his marvelous bridges, Marconi with his wireless telegraphy and telephony, Edison and Tesla with their electric and electrifying discoveries, or any of the renowned political reformers of the day, with all their futile schemes for turning this world into a terrestrial paradise. Friends, if you wish to be really, permanently, eternally useful, walk with God.

7. But there is a still better result than this from walking with God, *we please God*. Before his translation Enoch had this testimony borne to him that he "was well-pleasing to God" (Heb. 11:5, RV). This is more than to be useful. God wants our company, God wants us to walk with Him, and He is well-pleased when we do. God is more concerned that we walk with Him than that we work for Him. Martha was taken up with her service for her Lord, but Mary was taken up with her Lord Himself, and He testified that Mary had chosen the better part. It is quite possible today to be so occupied with our work for God that we forget Him, for whom we work. If we would please Him we should first see to it that we walk with him.

8. There is one result of walking with God still left to be mentioned, that is, *God's eternal companionship*. "Enoch walked with God:

and he was not; *for God took him.*" The man who walks on earth with God, God will sooner or later take to be with Himself forever. "If any man serve me," says Christ, "let him follow me; and where I am there shall also my servant be." If we do not walk with God on earth, we are not likely to live with God in heaven. If we do not care to cultivate His society now, we may be sure that He will not take us to be in His society forever.

III. How to Enter into a Walk with God

These eight immeasurably precious results come from walking with God: abounding joy, abiding peace, spiritual enlightenment, purity of heart and life, beauty of character, eminent usefulness, pleasing God, God's eternal companionship. Do we not all then long to walk with Him? To come then face to face with the great practical question, what must we do that we ourselves may enter into this joyous, blessed walk with Him. The question can be plainly and simply answered.

1. First of all we must *trust in the atoning blood of Christ.* "By faith," the record reads, "Enoch was translated" (Heb. 11:5; cf. v. 4). Comparing this with what is said immediately before about Abel, we see that the faith by which he pleased God and was translated was faith in what God said about the blood. God is holy, and we are sinners. Sin separates, as a deep and impassable chasm between us and Him. There can be no walk with Him until sin is put away and the chasm thus bridged, and it is the blood, and the blood alone, that puts away sin (Heb. 9:22). It is vain for us to attempt to cultivate the presence of God until we have accepted the provision that God Himself has made for putting away sin from between us and Himself. Indeed, if we have any real thought of God's holiness and our sinfulness there could be no joy, but only agony, in fellowship with Him, unless our sin was covered up, washed away, blotted out by the blood. There are many today who are spurning the blood and still attempting to walk with God. Vain attempt! It is utterly impossible.

2. If we would walk with God *we must obey God.* Jesus said, "If a man love me, he will keep my word: and my Father will love him, and we will come unto him, and make our abode with him" (John 14:23, RV). Obedience to God, absolute surrender to His will, is necessary if we are to walk with Him. We cannot walk with God unless we go His

His way. Two cannot walk together unless they be agreed (Amos 3:3). There are many who once knew the presence of God every day and every hour. They know it no longer. The old and heavenly joy has faded from their lives. They wonder why it is. Ah! there is no mystery—disobedience. Come back, get right with God, surrender anew absolutely to His will.

3. There is but one thing more to say. *If we would walk with God, we must cultivate the thought of His presence.* As Nicholas Hermann, or Brother Lawrence, put it, we must "practice the presence of God" constantly. Call to mind the fact that God is with you when you are about your work. Often say to yourself, "God is with me." When you lie down at night say, "God is with me." If you wake at night remember "God is here with me." So in all the relations and experiences of life. There are four great aids to this: First, the study of God's Word. When we open this Book we realize, or ought to realize, that God Himself is speaking to us. Second, prayer. In prayer we come face to face with God. Third, thanksgiving. In intelligent and specific thanksgiving to God He is more real to us than even in petition. Fourth, worship. In worship we bow before God and contemplate Himself. Oh, how near He gets at such a time. It is the Holy Spirit who will make our walk with God true and real. It is in connection with the coming of the Spirit that Christ speaks of His own manifestation of Himself to us and of the coming of the Father and of Himself to be with us (John 14:16–18, 21, 23). Look then to God Himself by His Spirit to make His presence known and felt.

Brethren, shall we walk with God? God is saying to each of us today, "Come, take a walk with me." If we accept the wondrous invitation, He will lead us on as long as we will let Him, and some day it will be true of us, as someone has quaintly said of Enoch, we will walk so far with God we will not come back, and so shall we ever be with the Lord.

Study Questions

1. What does it mean to walk with God?
2. What are the results of walking with God?
3. How do we enter into a walk with God?